A Guide to Independent Living

A GUIDE TO IN

DEPENDENT LIVING

Butterick Publishing

Editor
Barbara Weiland

Associate Editor
Elinor Dolgin

COVER DESIGN BY WINIFRED YOUNG
BOOK DESIGN BY BOB ANTLER

Library of Congress Catalog Card Number 75-9308
ISBN Number 0-88421-022-7

Copyright © 1975 by Butterick Publishing
161 Sixth Avenue   New York, New York 10013

A Division of American Can Company

All rights reserved. No part of this book may be reproduced in any form or by any electronic or mechanical means, including information storage and retrieval systems, without permission in writing from the publisher, except by a reviewer who may quote brief passages in a review.

PRINTED IN U. S. A.

First Printing, May 1975
Second Printing, February 1976
Third Printing, January 1977

FOREWORD

You are embarking on the adventure of a lifetime, the exhilarating era of establishing your own lifestyle independent of parents and family. It is an opportunity to be who you are and to decide just what you want from life. Now, you can find the "nuts and bolts" information on how to actually live on your own in "A Guide to Independent Living." It gives the whole story—facts that will help you make independent life a rich and fulfilling experience.

This modern, comprehensive book covers all aspects of practical living from finding and furnishing a place to live, to buying a car, from food shopping, to wardrobe planning, to surviving a visit from parents.

A Guide to Independent Living is the result of extensive research including interviews with young people, both single and newly married, who have experienced the joys, dilemmas, and rewards of independence.

The Editors

CONTENTS

Foreword v

1 SINGLE IS SUPER 1
The Single Years 1
Becoming Yourself 2
Away We Go 3
The Nuts and Bolts 4

2 NECESSITIES OF LIFE: SHELTER 5
Finding a Place to Live 5
Apartment Scorecard 7
Apartment Profiles 10
Movers and Moving 11
Roommates 14
Household Essentials 16
Keeping up with Housekeeping 18
Decorating Your Apartment 19
Planning the Decor 22
Apartment Greenery 24
For Security Reasons 28

3 NECESSITIES OF LIFE: FOOD — 33
Nutrition — 33
Dieting — 35
Calories Count — 36
Food Shopping — 45
Kitchen Talk — 80
Safety in the Kitchen — 88
Kitchen Abbreviations and Measures — 91
Outdoor Cooking — 93

4 NECESSITIES OF LIFE: CLOTHING — 94
Wardrobe Psychology — 94
Developing a Wardrobe — 95
Labels — 99
Taking Care of Your Wardrobe — 102

5 FINANCIAL AND LEGAL NITTY GRITTY — 115
Managing Your Money — 115
Banking: The Basics — 119
Credit — 125
Insurance — 138
Investments — 141
Taxes — 145
Legalities — 150

6 SOCIAL LIFE — 155
The Art of Entertaining — 155
Places to Go and People to Meet — 167

7 AT YOUR LEISURE — 174
Travel — 174
Recreation — 190

8 SINGLES' SUNDRIES — 194
Pets — 194
Buying a Car — 200
Surviving a Visit From Parents — 203
Career Opportunities — 204

9 TAKING CARE OF YOURSELF 206
Finding a Physician 206
Dental Care 208
One Final Word 209
Index 211

SINGLE IS SUPER

The Single Years

It usually happens less than a decade after the first awkward days of peach fuzz and training bras. Apron strings untied, a new generation of single adults puts to sea for what should be the adventure of a lifetime. Ahead are the single years, an exhilarating era of independence, a time of decision and self-government.

The first moments, if not years, are most deeply affected by upbringing. From earlier times when parents or guardians called most of the shots, comes a single person's first repertoire of resourcefulness. It's good for openers. Now you must add to it to suit your own lifestyle.

This is why *Single is Super*. Look at it as a period of self-sculpture, an exquisite opportunity to become yourself. There may be sudden revelations like a change in political views or a realization that you make better lasagne than your mother, and only after three cracks at it! Don't worry about it. In an atmosphere of mutual respect this isn't heresy, it's individuality! You're entitled to it just like everyone else.

Becoming Yourself

Single life is a time when you should become very much aware of yourself. There is no one quite like you. Imagine that. Not even a *chip off the old block* is a carbon copy. We can multiply but not duplicate ourselves. And with attitudes, outlooks and social environments changing and adjusting from one era to the next, young adults are expected to have new ideas and approaches to their own lives and to society.

Self-recognition is crucial because when you know *who* you are you can determine *where* you should be going. The alternative could well be an overdose of the middle age *ifs*. A two car garage hangover without an antidote. Too often people speak of their past youth as if it were a misguided bowling ball. *If only I could have it back!* (Sorry, no slipsies.) *If I had only graduated. If I hadn't gotten pregnant right away*. . . . The saddest commentary, the forbidden epitaph, is that a person didn't get to know himself or herself until it was too late to enjoy the pleasure of his or her company.

Self-recognition, what an experience to miss out on! It's the most sublime form of discovery, one that will give you perspective for the rest of your life.

Begin by taking inventory. Once you sort out your assets and liabilities (nobody's even near perfect) you will have cultivated the most important friend a person can have. Yourself! Based on this marvelous realization you can develop a sense of purpose. But don't get discouraged if an instant *you* doesn't materialize overnight. Relax, it's not supposed to happen that way. After all, it took you nine months to be born, over a decade to get a good case of acne, and eighteen years to be legally declassified as an infant.

Away We Go

There are times when it's absolutely invigorating to just wing it. In those sunkist days before you switch to a joint tax return, your income is completely at your disposal. Put it to good use. Spend it on yourself whenever you can. You may have heard that traveling is an education. Well, it can be sheer pleasure, too, and it doesn't have to cost you an arm and a leg, as you will see later on in this book.

Think about your wardrobe, too. When you can, dress the way you feel. Being comfortable with yourself and pleased with what you see in the mirror will make you radiate. Expect some quick changes. With each new ounce of individuality there will be some restyling. If you're a clothes hoarder, check your closet after a year. Chances are the *oldies* will no longer be the *goodies*.

Develop a respect for your *place* or apartment, too. It's really a form of self-respect, you know. The dormitory days are over. You have your own home now! There are many economical home furnishings buys and do-it-yourself ideas which we will get into soon. Take advantage of them.

The sport of single life, of course, needs to be balanced. Independent living has to be realistic. In fact it rarely works out the way you imagined it when you were in school. But there's so much to look forward to. So, be optimistic. A bright outlook is one of the not-so-secret ingredients of a successful life. The other part of the recipe is planning.

Everyone wants to be somebody. Well, you can't be anybody if you don't set your mind to it. Establish goals for yourself and go after them without delay. Remember, it's possible to procrastinate yourself all the way to an *iffy* middle age.

Set up timetables for yourself, check them regularly and rate your progress as often as you can. Give yourself a chance. We hear that Rome wasn't built in a day. Neither was General Motors, Disneyworld or Howard Cosell. Keep active; avoid stagnation.

Remain flexible, too. As you develop, so will new possibilities and potentials. You're going to hit a few potholes. Just fasten your seat belt. You can take a jolt better than anyone! Be introspective (self-recognition). Some of your best conversations can be with yourself.

The Nuts and Bolts

There's all sorts of romance in single life. There's the rhythm of your own pace. Quiet mornings with the Sunday papers. The carbonated good life. Meeting new people and updating old friends. Giving a damn all the time. Getting away from it all.

Enjoyment for the most part comes naturally to a single person. The basics have to be learned.

If you're apartment hunting for the first time, then you should know what to look for and how to tell a good deal from a bad one. When you begin to make money and spend it you must develop a system to budget it. There are necessities to purchase, supermarkets to explore, clogged drains that need fixing.

Nuts and bolts facts. They can save you time and money, prevent mistakes, help you manage every aspect of your life. Now they're at your fingertips . . . .

NECESSITIES OF LIFE: SHELTER

Finding a Place to Live

This is the first step to independence. It's a giant-sized one, not to be underestimated and only to be taken after you've analyzed what's available in terms of your requirements and current market values.

There are several immediate sources of apartment information. One is all it takes, but if you're moving into a high priority area where apartments are hard to get, we recommend that you tap at least a couple of sources simultaneously.

Friends. Very often the grapevine turns up the most interesting finds, so ask friends to keep an ear to the ground and an eye out for a vacancy. Let them know what you have in mind, size of apartment, maximum rent, general location. But keep it a bit loose; inflexibility will reduce the number of leads. It's always better to have too many than too few. And you never know what will strike you. People interested in high-rise buildings have been known to fall in love with two-flight walk-ups.

Newspaper Ads. This is the most obvious source and often the most productive. Sunday editions are usually the best and some of them can be purchased on Saturday night. Buy your copy as early as possible especially if apartments are at a premium in your area. Number availabilities in order of preference and pursue them with full speed.

In some communities there are special rental periodicals published for apartment hunters. They're inexpensive and can be helpful.

Real Estate Agents. It's their business to know what's available. And frequently they have *unlisted* availabilities. As a central source of information they'll save you unnecessary leg work, too. But they cost money. The fee is usually the equivalent of one month's rent or 10% of your yearly rent.

Doormen. If you're interested in an apartment building that has doorman service, make a list of those buildings that interest you, then check with each doorman. You will find that most of them are helpful. If there's a vacancy or an expected vacancy in a building, they can direct you to someone who can fill you in on the details. Sunday is the best day to get a doorman's attention. There are no mail or package deliveries to distract him and tenant activity is minimal.

Bulletin Boards. They're not a primary source. Nevertheless, they're worth checking. Some supermarkets and employers have them. And don't forget to check bulletin boards in school libraries and college campus buildings.

Apartment Scorecard

When you begin to visit prospective apartments, you must be able to rate them quickly and realistically. Here is what to consider and what to look for:

Size. The number of rooms is dependent on your needs and budget. It's ideal, of course, to have an apartment with a separate bedroom.
 In studio apartments (also called efficiencies) all the living is done in one room. Yet there are ways to create areas of privacy within a studio. So don't discount them. The opposite extreme is the apartment with many rooms. If the price is right it's hard to turn down such an opportunity. But don't forget that each room will require interior decoration and that means money.
 Room size is always a definite consideration. Tiny rooms can be a problem. If they can't accommodate ordinary furniture sizes, your lifestyle surely will be cramped. You may even develop an apologetic attitude when entertaining guests. Avoid this kind of discomfort.

Light. Check to see what kind of sun exposure the apartment gets. Dark, gloomy apartments can be depressing. Plants won't like it either. If you're shown an apartment in the evening, it's a good idea to visit it again in the daytime before making a decision.

Fixtures. The plumbing, refrigerator and stove should be in good working condition. If they're not, make sure that they will be repaired or replaced before you sign the lease. If the refrigerator and stove don't come with the apartment (sounds archaic but it can happen) make sure you can afford them. More importantly, judge whether the apartment is worth this kind of expense. If it is, you may be able to find some good secondhand buys.

Ventilation. In the absence of air conditioning, cross ventilation can provide relief during warm spells. If you want air conditioning and it is not provided by the landlord, make sure the building can handle the electrical load before you invest in a unit. Because walls are natural barriers, one air conditioner cannot be expected to cool a multi-room apartment. Therefore, locate it where it will do the most good. Our recommendation is the bedroom. A good night's sleep comes first.

Soundproofing. When you inspect an apartment, listen for noises from without (traffic) and from within (upstairs neighbors and next-door neighbors). You can get a true indication of neighbor noise in the early evening when most people are home. If you can hear them clearly, then they will be able to hear you clearly. This could be a problem when you entertain. To cut down on noise distractions, choose an apartment located away from elevators, stairwells, and incinerator chutes.

Building Maintenance. During every tenancy there are times when repairs will be needed. You can get an indication of what kind of service to expect for your apartment by visually inspecting the condition of the lobby, hallways, stairwells or vestibules. If these areas are in a below par state, chances are apartment repairs won't come easily.

Neighborhood and Security. The national crime rate has risen. Major metropolitan areas have been especially hard hit. Thus, it is essential that you evaluate the neighborhood and building security. Streets should be well lit. Building entrances should be locked or attended by doormen. Ask friends about the reputation of the neighborhood. The local police station may be a good source of information about the area you're investigating.

Convenience. Day-to-day living can be helped or hindered by your apartment's location. Is it near public transportation? How much will it cost? If you are moving into the suburbs and you work in the city, how much is the commuter fare? Do you need a car to get around? Do you want to be near supermarkets, cleaners, and shops?

Miscellaneous Building Services. Is there allowance for package deliveries in your building? A package room is ideal but certainly not a must. However, there should be some assurance that packages delivered when you're not at home will be accepted and held for you. Often the superintendent of an apartment building will be responsible for this service.

Check storage space, too. Some buildings have storage rooms. Others will offer space in basements. Check it for security. If it's located away from your apartment, it's a good idea to check it periodically. If such space exists, determine beforehand if it is cost free. If you're a bicycle rider, make a specific inquiry about bike storage. In some metropolitan buildings they're now charging a garage fee for bikes.

Lease. Most critical is the lease. It's a contract that both parties (landlord and tenant) must honor. So read it carefully. If you're uncertain about any clauses or terminology *ask questions,* and don't sign anything until all questions have been satisfactorily answered. Most leases are standard forms. Thus, if you have reached a verbal agreement with the landlord or agent about anything (e.g. they've agreed to replace the refrigerator at no cost to you) this will require a rider or supplementary clause.

Some questions to ask at lease signing time are: Are gas, heat and electricity included in your rent? If you have a pet or plan to acquire one, will this be allowed? Will you be allowed to sublet? Will your landlord paint the apartment before you move in, and how often thereafter will it be painted (three years is standard)? If you paint the apartment or make other improvements, will the landlord pay for the materials? Does the management employ an exterminator? The term of the lease must be weighed, too. If there's a strong possibility that you'll be moving (job relocation, for example) in the near future a short lease could be preferable. However, rents are always on the rise. Thus, if relocation doesn't materialize and you decide to renew your lease at the end of the year, expect an increase. For this reason some real estate experts recommend a two or three year lease with a sublet arrangement. Call it a hedge against inflation. It guarantees you a fixed rent for a longer period. If relocation calls before the lease has expired then you can resort to subletting. But be very careful in screening sublet prospects. If they default in rent payment, you, the original tenant by virtue of your lease, can be held responsible for the subtenant's unpaid rent. It's like cosigning a loan. So be selective. The best prospects are people who you know to be reliable and honest.

When you sign a lease, you will probably be asked to pay a security deposit. It may be as little as $50 or as much as two months' rent. Some states require that this deposit be put into a savings account and the interest paid to you annually. Be sure to ask about this deposit. Is it refundable and under what conditions? How long will it take to get it back once you vacate the apartment? Is it security against damages to the apartment or security against default on payment of rent?

Apartment Profiles

Apartment Building vs. Two-Family Houses. Actually they're not rivals. But they do represent two different lifestyles. The apartment building or garden apartment complex is perhaps more impersonal but offers a higher degree of privacy. Although you must always be considerate of neighbors, sharing a two-family residence requires more sensitivity. So, before signing a lease for this type of apartment, get acquainted with the other occupant (very often it's the owner) to determine whether or not you will be compatible.

Singles' Apartments. Some people consider them frivolous. Yet there are advantages, especially for outgoing individuals. A community spirit prevails constantly. Single tenants share lounges, swimming pools, saunas, bars, volleyball courts. There are lots of social events. Rents are often reasonable, too. The general age range is 25 to 35. Thus, tenants tend to have similar values and outlooks, a factor that often leads to quick friendships. However, if chuminess is not your style, avoid this kind of rental.

Movers and Moving

Moving must be planned with a sense of efficiency and economy. Begin by selecting a very reliable mover. Ask experienced friends for recommendations. If that doesn't work, check with the Better Business Bureau or local consumer affairs groups.

To accurately estimate the cost of the move, your mover will need to see everything that's going. Some people outsmart themselves by not showing everything to the estimator. Then, at moving time, they include the *missing* items in the shipment. This increases moving time and cargo weight. Result: the final bill exceeds the estimate. And you must pay it since an estimate is not a binding contract.

A visit from your mover also gives you the opportunity to nail down specific pick up and delivery dates and times. You should also point out any pieces of property that need special attention. Paintings and mirrors are good examples. They need to be cartoned.

A good mover will give you a copy of the *ICC Summary of Information for Shippers of Household Goods*. On the cover of this 33 page brochure, it says "Read this booklet: it could save you money, time and unnecessary aggravation." Quite true. All the essentials are covered, from selecting a mover to filing claims. There are chapters on money-saving tips, bills of lading, storage in transit, and more. If your mover doesn't offer you a copy, by all means ask for one. You can also obtain one by writing the Interstate Commerce Commission, Washington D.C. 20423. Identify the book as Form BOp 103, Revised 1974.

Breakage can happen even with the best movers. If it does, a mover is liable for only 60 cents per pound per article, hardly enough to cover any damage done to valuable furniture or glassware. If you're not being reimbursed for losses by an employer or associate, you should invest in insurance.

Another important point: movers are not liable for cash, jewelry, securities, coin collections, and similar possessions, so take them with you. In fact, if you're moving to a new apartment in the same area, it's a good idea to personally move your more precious possessions by automobile. If you don't own a car, perhaps a friend does.

If you are moving to a new city, your goods are covered by your mover's insurance for 180 days. After that, you must take new insurance to cover it in permanent storage.

There are many extra services offered by the better movers. Appliances can be detached before moving and hooked up at your new apartment. Although movers won't take pets, frozen foods, or plants on the van, they can arrange for air freighting them to the new destination. You can get expedited, speedy delivery—but it will cost two or three times the normal cost.

Some quick tips on moving efficiency:

1. Extra stops cost extra money. If you have belongings in more than one place, get them all together for a single pick up.
2. All cartons should be marked and numbered. This will save time and eliminate confusion at your new destination. Each carton should be clearly labeled and color coded by the room (red for kitchen, blue for living room, yellow for bedroom).
3. You may arrive at your new apartment before the movers (especially if you're moving from one city to another). So come prepared. Bring along a special carton containing things that will tide you over until everything is settled. Some suggested items include a small coffee pot, an ashtray (if you smoke), aspirin, first aid items, a drinking glass, and a pillow and sleeping bag just in case the movers don't arrive at the specified time.
4. Don't pack flammables—cleaning fluids, turpentine or aerosols. Under intense heat they can explode.
5. Check the mover's household goods descriptive inventory list before the van starts rolling toward your new destination. And double check all rooms, closets, drawers, shelves.
6. When your belongings are delivered, check them against your inventory list.
7. If anything is lost or damaged make note of it on the inventory list *before* you sign it. Then file a claim for damage or loss as soon as possible.
8. Once you know where you're moving, contact the telephone company for the installation of your phone. Installation schedules can vary from one local telephone company to the next. You will be asked for a deposit which will be returned to you with interest in a year.
9. When you move into your new apartment, make sure you don't walk into darkness. Ask the landlord

or superintendent to have the gas and/or electricity turned on by the time you arrive. Sometimes a security deposit is required for these utilities.

If you don't want to use or simply can't afford a professional mover, then rely completely on friends. Although moving is heavy work it can have some lighthearted moments. You might even consider a little celebration after you've completed the move. Have some beverages on hand at your new apartment. Perspiration and moving go together. And so does a thirst.

Roommates

Sharing an apartment with a roommate or roommates has its pluses and minuses. It provides companionship and a situation where responsibilities and expenditures for rent, utilities, and food can be split. On the other hand, there is a loss of privacy and need for some compromises in order to achieve harmony.

A roommate may become a necessity rather than a matter of choice. You may want to live in a high rent district but can't cope with the rent on your own. You may feel safer in numbers especially in areas where the incidence of crime is on the rise.

Whatever the reason, you should know each roommates' individual needs, personality, living habits and schedules before you sign a lease. Neil Simon's play, "The Odd Couple," is a theatrically hilarious story about two divorced men who share an apartment but in real life it would be disastrous over a long period of time.

The old cliché, "you don't know a person until you live with him or her," is very true, but your chances of successfully sharing an apartment with a roommate are considerably better if you know the person beforehand.

The longer the friendship the more accurately you will be able to gauge your potential compatibility as roommates. It would be helpful, too, if you've already had a sharing experience with a prospective roommate, e.g. college dormitory, summer home, traveling together.

Once you've chosen your roommate, immediately discuss the realities of maintaining a household. List your strengths and weaknesses. One may be a great cook; the other may like housecleaning. If so, divide those responsibilities accordingly. But often times it is not that clearcut. Thus you may have to take turns shouldering certain responsibilities no matter how incapable both of you may be. Don't let chores go unattended. An otherwise good relationship can unravel under these circumstances. Be definite about responsibilities. It will preclude accusations and misunderstandings. Learn to compromise. Always consult one another over major household decisions. A unilateral purchase of a piece of furniture or a pet could lead to a serious argument. Make arrangements about the food bill. If your eating habits are similar, splitting the food bill is the wisest decision. But if your schedules and eating habits don't coordinate, you can avoid problems and arguments by maintaining separate food cabinets and areas in the refrigerator.

Whatever your joint lifestyle, have an agreement about it before you start living it. And don't be afraid to review it if you feel your roommate is slipping. If you're the guilty party, don't feel offended. Talk it out. A few adjustments may be in order, particularly in the early stages of sharing an apartment.

Individual schedules are important, too. If you're planning to entertain, let your roommate know about it in advance. If you must take an unexpected trip, leave word as to where you will be and when you expect to return.

It's not necessary to inform your roommate of every detail in your life. Nor should you expect a total revelation from him or her. But be empathetic toward each other.

When problems arise—and they always do—advice from a roommate can be most helpful.

If things just don't work out, face up to it as soon as you are convinced that your differences are irreconcilable. Take a deep breath, put aside any hard feelings, and discuss your options. If a move is dictated, determine who will move, what will be taken and when the move is most feasible.

There may be other reasons for moving, too. One roommate may have to relocate because of job opportunity. Or there may be a marriage. In any event, the person leaving should give sufficient notice. The remaining roommate will need time to find a replacement.

Household Essentials

To make your household function properly, you must equip it with certain necessities. The following list can serve as a shopping guide. Tailor it, of course, to suit your own needs or preferences. But don't overlook items that fail to catch your fancy. Even if you're not planning to cook for yourself, you must think ahead to times when you'll be entertaining friends or perhaps family. And, as every single learns, there's no such thing as a non-cook. There will be occasions when you must be self-sufficient.

Start with a service for four in dishware and flatware. You can always add more later. You'll also need glasses, kitchen utensils, linens and other general items. Read through the list and use your judgment.

Flatware. Forks, knives, teaspoons, soup spoons, serving spoons.

Dishware. Dinner plates, salad plates, soup plates or bowls, cups and saucers (you could use mugs and save on the saucers), dessert bowls.

Glassware. There are many styles and many price ranges. Inexpensive goblets for red wine are a good idea. They work well for serving anything from orange juice to Alka Seltzer. They can even be used for certain desserts such as puddings, ice cream, sherbet, berries. You may want to get a dozen or so. They'll come in handy for parties.

Kitchen Utensils. Set of knives, wooden mixing spoons, rubber spatula, can opener, tongs, funnel, mixing bowls, cutting/carving board, colander, strainer, measuring cups, measuring spoons, kitchen tool set which includes a large spoon, flat spatula, ladle, large fork, and pancake turner. It should also include a wall mount.

Pots and Pans. Roasting pan, saucepan, frying pans (1 small, 1 large), tea kettle, coffee maker, dutch oven, casserole dish, baking pans.

Holloware. Platter, salad bowl, butter dish, salt & pepper shakers, ashtrays, pitcher, serving trays.

Bed Linens. Two or three sets of sheets (fitted and flat), one winter-weight blanket (unless climate dictates differently), one or two pillows, two pillow cases for each pillow, bedspread.

Bath Linens. Four bath towels, four hand towels, four washcloths, bath mat, shower curtain.

Kitchen Linen. Dish towels, pot holders.

General. Ironing board, iron, hamper, canister set, garbage pail, wastebasket, step stool, dish drainer, toaster, bottle opener, cork screw.

Other Essentials . . . First Aid and Medicine Cabinet Items. Adhesive bandages, first aid cream, sterile pads, first aid tape, thermometer, rubbing alcohol, antiseptic soap, aspirin or equivalent, boric acid eye wash. Although not for the medicine cabinet, you should also have a hot water bottle and ice bag.

Keeping Up With Housekeeping

You don't have to keep your home sterilized but maintaining it so that it's fairly clean and orderly will make life more pleasant. Establishing a routine makes cleaning easier and less time-consuming. One simple routine is to envision your apartment as the face of a clock and clean it clockwise, starting at twelve and ending there. This method will eliminate a lot of extra steps.

How much time you spend at home will determine how much cleaning you'll have to do. If you eat out most of the time, obviously dishes won't pile up. In any event there are some basic chores that need attention no matter how much you may dislike doing them.

Here is a thumbnail guide to cleaning. Follow it according to what does or doesn't apply to you. If you don't get around to doing all the chores don't panic. The cleaning part of your life is mainly for your sake.

Everyday. Make bed, hang up all clothes. Empty ashtrays, garbage. Wash, rinse, dry and put away all dishes and glassware. Wipe out bathtub, sink.

Once a Week. Dust window sills, picture frames, knickknacks. Vacuum. Polish furniture, wash vinyl floors. Clean windows, mirrors. Change bedding, replace towels. Clean bathroom, defrost refrigerator, clean oven (ugh!).

To maintain your apartment properly and make cleaning as easy as possible you should have a full complement of cleaning aids. Here are some suggestions.

Cleaning Aids. Pails, rubber gloves, sponges, soft cloths, steel wool, toilet bowl brush, upholstery brush, vacuum, floor buffer, mop, broom, ammonia, enamel polish, floor waxes, furniture polish, household detergent, oven cleaner, spray disinfectant, scouring powder, toilet bowl cleaner, window cleaner, dish detergent.

There are also seasonal chores such as carpet cleaning and floor polishing which may require special equipment. Borrow or rent what you need and follow instructions.

If you honestly feel that you can't cope with the housekeeping responsibilities but refuse to live under mountains of dirt, consider getting some outside help. It sounds more expensive than it really is. Someone could come on a weekly or semi-monthly basis. You may have friends who know of a good cleaning person. If you live in a building that has doorman service, ask the day man. Very often he will be able to recommend a good cleaning person who's already doing work in your building.

The hourly cost can vary. A one bedroom apartment can be cleaned within four hours on a weekly basis. This should also include having your machine laundry done — that is if there are facilities in your building or at least close by. One caution: even if you hire someone on this basis you will still have to do some straightening between cleaning sessions. Think it out and judge whether it would be worth the money or whether it would be wise to give cleaning a second chance.

Decorating Your Apartment

Your apartment is a reflection of your personality, your sense of taste, your attitude toward life and toward yourself. A well decorated apartment is a source of pleasure. It should give you a sense of comfort, especially after a hard day. And it should give your guests a sense of warmth and welcome . . . also a feeling of respect for you.

If you're starting from scratch, here are the bare necessities to put on your home furnishings shopping list.

Living Room. Sofa or sofa bed (best for a studio apartment), armchair, coffee table, end tables, rug, lamps, shelves.

Bedroom. Bed, mattress and box spring, night tables, chest, lamp, rug.

Dining Area. Table, chairs.

Other Comforts. Clock, mirror, radio, TV, stereo.

You needn't or shouldn't want to buy everything all at once. It takes time to select and accumulate those pieces that are right for you. Enjoy the experience. You can buy new or secondhand pieces. In either case always shop for a bargain. It may take longer but the results will be worth it. Insist on quality for the price you pay.

When shopping for new furnishings, check ads, ask friends about best buys. Sometimes you will uncover wholesale furniture outlets. And by comparison shopping you'll come to recognize a true discount. It's also wise to make major purchases during traditional sale periods. According to the Retail Merchants Association, May is the sale month for indoor furniture, June is the sale month for bedding and floor coverings, and January is *White Sale* month.

Buying secondhand furniture and accessories can be fun and economical. There are great finds at auctions, flea markets, garage sales, antique shops, used furniture stores. Before buying, however, you should get some experience. Determine what interests you, then check prices and listen to bids (at auctions). In no time at all you'll know what a real bargain is and where the best bargain can be found. Prices don't lie. If two items are very similar in workmanship and condition, the cheaper one is the better buy.

Auctions. They are very appealing to bargain hunters. Not only can you get a good buy, but the bidding system is an exciting form of competition. Check the conditions of sale beforehand. They will either be printed clearly in the catalogue or read to you by the auctioneer. A final bid is usually irrevocable. So it's best to inspect all goods before the auction begins. If you're satisfied with the condition of certain pieces, then bid on them within your means. Prior to auction write down the maximum prices you're willing to pay and don't exceed them.

Flea Markets. It's great to poke around at a flea market. Hundreds of them are held throughout the country all year long. If you're interested in locating the best ones in your area, ask friends and check the newspaper's marketplace classified ads. A flea market is a potpourri. Usually you'll find everything from old magazines and license plates to antique clocks and jewelry. If you get the urge, it's permissible to haggle over price.

Garage and Rummage Sales. Junking can be a great sport and this is another form of it. To find these sales look in the classified section of your newspaper. You may be surprised at the bargains. Since these sales are not normally conducted by professional dealers, prices are often lower than they should be.

Antique Shops. Good antique stores have great collections of beautiful and interesting items. They're well worth a visit. However, if they're located in high income neighborhoods, chances are their prices will be more expensive than used furniture stores, thrift shops, or auctions. Nevertheless, window shopping is free of charge. And you never know when or where a bargain will appear.

Used Furniture Stores. They're a must for an incorrigible junker. Check the phone book for the location of the Salvation Army, Goodwill Industry outlets, and others. Stocks vary from month to month, so you should visit these sources regularly.

For the true junker there are many special interest publications. A few are:

>*Book for Collectors*, Free from R. J. Beck Company, P. O. Box #1, Huntertown, Indiana 46748.
>
>*Collector's Weekly*, a weekly newspaper covering Illinois, Indiana, Kentucky, Michigan, Ohio, Tennessee, western Pennsylvania and Wisconsin. P. O. Box 90, Knightstown, Indiana 46148.
>
>*Collectible Trends*, a newsletter from 4284 West 143rd, Cleveland, Ohio 44135.

Planning the Decor

Before you actually begin to buy home furnishings you should ask your landlord for a floor plan of your apartment. Make a couple of tracings of it or have copies made at a quick copy service center.

Now begin to experiment with furniture shapes. Draw them to scale so that there are no miscalculations. If something is not in the scale of your floor plan, areas of your apartment may end up being too empty or too cluttered. Be sure to plan for future purchases.

There are several general rules to keep in mind when planning your decor on paper.

1. Situate furniture so that traffic patterns are not blocked. Passage from one room to the next, or from one area to the next, should not be hindered.
2. In rooms where people will congregate (living room, den) arrange furniture so that conversation will

flow freely. If chairs are removed or isolated from conversation circles, they lose their purpose and create a vacuum.
3. Balance the furniture. If furniture is unevenly distributed, chances are you won't be using the space to its fullest advantage.
4. Lighting should be well distributed, too, and keyed to furniture or objects of interest.

When you begin to select your furnishings, coordinate colors and patterns very carefully. It's virtually impossible to remember the exact depth or tone of any color, so take swatches with you when you shop. Place paint chips and fabric samples side by side. Always ask a home furnishings salesperson for a snip of the fabric or fabrics that you like. Then as you move from upholstery to floor coverings you can coordinate colors and patterns perfectly.

These are just tips. We suggest you read up on the art of interior design before you begin to purchase. Libraries and book stores have lots of books on the subject and there are many decorating magazines on the newsstands. Also look for magazines specifically devoted to apartment living.

Room settings in better stores can be a source for ideas, too. And if you really want to make a study of interior design, check to see if courses are being given at local schools, YMCA's, and YWCA's.

If you are still very unsure about what to select and how to put it all together, you may need outside help. If a friend has great taste, he or she may be the answer. If not, you might consider the services of a professional interior designer. There are two basic choices: private designers and department store staff designers.

The private designer handles fewer clients. So his or her service is usually more concentrated and personal. There is also a greater freedom of selection since you will not be restricted to choosing one store's merchandise.

Private designers also tend to plunge more deeply into the assignment and will follow through by visiting your apartment, even supervising work crews if it comes to that.

There are ways that a private interior designer can be paid: (1) he or she buys at wholesale and sells to you at retail, keeping the difference as profit; (2) he or she buys for you at wholesale, charges you this price and adds on a percentage of the total cost as a fee, (3) he or she estimates the assignment and quotes a fixed fee. Get the method of payment straight before you commission any work.

With a department store designer you pay retail prices but, of course, must make all purchases within his or her store. Thus, you must be careful that your apartment doesn't acquire a stereotyped *department store* look. Nevertheless, the better in-store designers can be helpful — if they're not inundated with other assignments.

Many department store designers are salaried. But some work on a commission or part salary/part commission basis. Occasionally this type of designer may tend to sell merchandise more than counsel clients. So if you have a strict budget, be firm about it.

Apartment Greenery

In a world that often seems too automated, too manufactured, more and more people are becoming plant lovers. What a refreshing phenomenon! Plants have special significance for apartment dwellers. In the absence of backyards or plots of land they represent the miracle of nature.

The best place to buy a plant is a store that specializes in them. The so-called bargains that you will find in supermarkets and cut-rate stores or from mail order firms are often poor specimens that have suffered through rough treatment and lack of care. It will take a green thumb and constant attention to insure their survival.

Successful plant specialists offer more of a variety than non-specialists. And they tend to be more knowledgeable about their care and the conditions that will best enhance their growth.

When shopping for plants your first consideration must be light. Your apartment can have two sources: artificial and natural. If you're interested in providing artificial light, invest some money in special fixtures or bulbs. But, if you're watching the budget, here's how to get the most out of the natural light available.

Evaluate your apartment. Most window areas provide three types of natural light: (1) no direct sun; (2) a limited amount of direct sun—maybe an hour or so; (3) full sun. Choose your plants accordingly (see chart which follows for suggestions). The healthiest plant will wither quickly in conditions that are not suited to its well-being.

REQUIRED LIGHT FOR SOME COMMON HOUSEPLANTS

No Direct Sun	Limited Direct Sun	Full Sun
Rubber Plant	Begonia	Geranium
Aspidistra	African Violet	Citrus
Sansevieria (for foliage)	Asparagus Fern	Sanseviera (for blossoms)
Maranta	Gloxinia	Verbena
Philodendron	Azalea	Euphorbia
Grape Ivy	Spider Plant	Grape Ivy
Fiddle-Leaf Fig	Rosary Vine	Coleus
Boston Fern	Grape Ivy	Rat-Tail Cactus
Bamboo Palm	Dieffenbachia	Aloe
Kentia Palm	Columnea	Aztec Lily
Pothos	Avocado	

Before buying a plant check it out thoroughly for pests (look under the leaves and at stem junctures). Pass up plants with unnatural blotched, speckled, or yellow leaves. Foliage should have a healthy, green character.

Ask your retailer about over watering. Overdoses can damage roots and ultimately cause deterioration of the entire plant. Since humidity can vary from apartment to apartment, some plants will dry out more quickly than expected. So periodically poke your finger into the pot. If the soil is dry, it's a sign your plant needs water. Always use tepid water. Cold water is a shocker to plants as well as people.

Morning is the recommended time for watering. Misting or spraying leaves should be done in the evening to simulate dew.

Most house plants need to be fertilized. Those that flower should be fed just as they begin to bloom and approximately every two weeks thereafter. Foliage plants only need fertilizing once a month or every six weeks during their growing season (usually October through March).

Ask your plant store specialist to recommend a fertilizer. Follow the package instructions carefully.

A plant needs to be transferred to a new pot if it has outgrown its present pot to the point where the roots can no longer expand. Transferring to a larger pot is known as *potting on.* You can help restore life in a plant that is withering in a large pot by transferring it to a smaller pot with rich new soil. This is called *potting back.* In any event, all plants should be repotted about every two years. New loose soil will help the roots feel more comfortable, a state that will assure a healthier, greener life.

To re-pot, just put one hand over the top of the old pot with the main stem of the plant between your middle and index fingers. Turn the pot upside down and knock it sharply against the edge of a table. This will loosen the pot from the soil enabling you to pull it off. Remove as much dirt as you can from between the roots and cut back any roots that appear to be broken or rotted. After placing a piece of broken pot over the drainage hole in the new pot to keep the soil from rushing out, pour enough sterilized potting soil into the pot so that when you perch the root ball on it lightly, it will be at least $3/4''$ from the bottom of the pot. Pour more fresh soil around the roots. Give the pot a couple of sharp raps to help settle the soil. Soil should be firmly packed. Then plunge the new planting into a bucket of tepid water for five minutes. Now a normal plant has its new home and needn't be moved for two years unless potting on or potting back becomes necessary.

Although most plants are relatively inexpensive you may want to find ways to save money in the process of increasing your indoor garden. One of the easiest ways and one which stimulates new friendships is to conduct a plant swap with friends or neighbors in your building. It's fun to exchange cuttings from healthy plants and to share ideas for displaying and lighting your plant collections.

Another way to save money on indoor gardens is to grow plants from seed and to try *garbage gardening.* Use the pit from a ripe avocado, seeds from citrus foods and grapes, or sprouts on sweet potatoes. To plant an avocado pit, first peel away the parchment-like covering. Then, cut a tiny slice from both ends. Prop the pit halfway into a glass of water using toothpicks stuck into the pit. Three should do it! When a healthy root system has developed and a $6''$ sprout has emerged from the top, plant in a pot $10''$ in diameter with half of the pit exposed. Then, cut the sprout back half its length. This won't hurt your fledgling plant; in fact, you'll have a healthier, bushier plant in the long run. During its first months of growth, it's a good idea to pinch away new leaves in every other new growth to encourage bushiness. Otherwise, you'll have a straight stalk with leaves waving from the top. It *is* possible to grow an avocado *tree* using this method.

Plant citrus seeds in a $6''$ pot filled with dirt to an inch below the top. Soak the dirt, then push about eight seeds into dirt about $1/4''$ deep. Keep in a sunny spot and keep evenly moist. When plants begin to crowd each other, transplant to individual pots. Citrus plants can grow to tree-size proportions and their blossoms have a light, enjoyable fragrance.

For a bushy sweet potato vine, choose a sweet potato with a live sprout. Suspend the potato in a container with the large end up and cover the bottom half with water. Keep well-watered and it will grow thick with vines in no time at all.

For real *green thumbs* a complete book on indoor gardening and house plants is a must! But, this will get you on your way to a happy life with healthy greenery to add color and beauty to your home.

For Security Reasons

Securing your entrances begins with the door itself, *then* the lock. If your front or rear doors have glass or wooden panels, the least skilled burglar can knock out a panel and enter.

Doors

The safest doors are made of hollow metal (another thing to check when you're apartment hunting).

A good door requires a snug-fitting frame. Steel is the best but a sturdy wooden frame is also good. If you have a weak door frame or a loose fitting door that your landlord won't repair, install a jimmy-guard. This is an L-shaped angle iron at least two feet long mounted on the frame opposite the lock. The guard will act as a lip protecting the latch and deadbolt from attack, even if the door and frame are spread apart. You can install a jimmy-guard yourself. Or, if you prefer, a locksmith can do it for a reasonable fee.

If your doors open outwards, their hinges are exposed.

They can be flanged with a hammer or by welding. Or, a set screw or flat-headed, self-tapping screw can be inserted through a portion of the hinge that is not exposed when the door is closed. You can find these items in a hardware store.

If you have a substantial door, then invest in a lock that will make it reasonably secure. One of the finest anti-burglar locks is the Medeco. The key is quite ordinary looking but the lock is extremely difficult to pick. The longer a burglar must work on a lock the greater is the risk of discovery. The key to a Medeco lock cylinder can be duplicated only by a locksmith who has invested $1750 in a special machine that can decode and cut Medeco keys.

Cylinders with tubular keys are recommended, too. Many burglars make fast work of flat-key cylinders by driving a heavy screwdriver into the key slot then twisting it with a vise grip. This is impossible with tubular key cylinders.

Give duplicate keys only to trusted neighbors or relatives. If you prefer not to give a duplicate to your superintendent (he's supposed to have one in case of fire), give him the name and phone number of the person(s) who has a duplicate.

Windows. There are two types of windows: accessible and reachable. Accessible windows are those at ground floor, off a porch, or facing a fire escape. Reachable windows are those that a burglar can reach but with some difficulty.

For reachable windows a carriage bolt is a good idea. It fits through a hole in the lower frame and into the cavity drilled in the upper frame. The window can be secured in a partially open position by drilling a second cavity higher up in the frame of the upper window. A carriage bolt is not exposed to attack by a hacksaw.

Accessible windows need extra protection. Accordian gates are effective for windows that require no access during a fire.

Make sure that your window frame is sturdy enough to hold the gate in place during an attack.

For windows that do require access during a fire, check out gates that will meet with local Fire Department regulations or standards.

If you feel that accordians or gates are too unsightly, there are manufacturers who make a laminated glass that resists breakthrough. Another alternative is a plastic named Lexan made by General Electric.

In Case of a Break-In. If you arrive home to find a door that appears to have been pried or forced, leave quietly without calling attention to yourself. Then telephone the police immediately. Do *not* re-enter your apartment until someone else can go in with you.

When or if you re-enter before the police arrive, do not disturb anything. Tell the police what has been taken and how much it's worth. Have your locks changed as soon as possible after a burglary.

If you are awakened at night by an intruder, do not scream or try to apprehend him. If he has a weapon, this kind of action may cause him to use it. Simply be still, memorize his description if possible and notify the police the minute he's gone.

Tips from the American Police and Fire Foundation include the following:

Burglary

▶ Keep doors, windows, and screens locked, day and night, home or away.

▶ Burn a light visible from the street at night at your doorway. When away leave a light burning, preferably with a timing device.

▶ Never allow strangers or solicitors in your home. Always ask for credentials first, then check them out by phone.

▶ Encourage your neighbors' cooperation in watching each other's homes when you or they are away.
▶ Arrange for a neighbor to pick up your mail or newspaper or temporarily discontinue newspaper service so that they do not accumulate—a sure sign that no one is home.
▶ Learn all you can about crime prevention techniques and cooperate fully with your local police.
▶ Notify your local police if you intend to be away for several days.

Fire

▶ *Do not* smoke in bed or allow small children to play with matches.
▶ Store all flammable liquids in a secure, UL approved container and in a well ventilated area.
▶ Keep your dwelling free of unnecessary clutter and trash. Good housecleaning reduces the risk of fire and enhances your chances of escape in case of fire.
▶ Make sure your home's electrical system is functioning properly. *Do not* overload circuits by plugging a lot of electrical appliances into one outlet.
▶ Drill young children and elderly people in proper escape routes.
▶ Learn all you can about your local fire unit and how it operates. Cooperation with fire officials is the best deterrent to unnecessary loss of life and property.
▶ Ask your local Fire Prevention Unit to inspect your home for potential fire hazards.

Common Sense Personal Safety Rules

▶ Don't walk alone at night in deserted parts of the city.
▶ Don't be an appeaser. If someone approaches you on the street, being friendly or diffident won't disarm him.

Ignore him and if he persists, tell him to get away or you'll call the police.

▶ Look around to see if you're being followed when approaching your building.

▶ Have your keys on hand so you won't be searching for them when you're about to open the door.

▶ If someone grabs you, or your belongings, scream or shout as loud as you can.

▶ Don't get on an elevator with someone suspicious-looking.

▶ If you're driving alone, lock the doors. Be sure to check the car before getting into it. It's easy for someone to hide in the back seat, especially at night. If you think someone is following you, drive straight to the local police station. Make sure all car doors are locked and windows are tightly closed. If the follower is still behind you when you reach the station, blow your horn until someone comes to help you.

Emergency Telephone Numbers. In case of sickness, injury, fire, or need for protection you should have the following emergency telephone numbers handy:

Police	Fire
Rescue Squad	Doctor
Hospital	Ambulance
Insurance	Utilities
Apartment Superintendent	Neighbor

NECESSITIES OF LIFE: FOOD

Nutrition

Most vitamins and minerals were discovered in this century. So it's not surprising that the great majority of people have become aware of nutrition only during the last thirty years. Publicity about it has been good. But occasionally, wittingly or unwittingly, it has been a source of misinformation and food fads. If you want the straight facts, get a standard guide to food values needed daily by writing to the National Academy of Sciences, National Research Council, Washington D.C. 20418. Ask for a copy of *Recommended Dietary Allowances*. Cost is $1. It's also available in libraries.

    In the meantime here is a basic daily nutritional guide for your reference. For nutritional purposes, foods can be divided into four basic groups. An adequate diet includes at least the minimum number of daily servings from each group. If you do hard physical work, you will need an extra portion. This holds true for pregnant women and those who are breast-feeding a baby.

	Recommended Daily Amounts	*Major Contribution*
Milk and Milk Foods: *Use fresh, canned, dried milk; cheeses; ice cream.*	Adults: 2 or more cups. Teenagers: 4 or more cups. Pregnant women: 4 or more cups. Nursing mothers: 6 or more cups.	Principal source of calcium for bones and teeth; also contains high quality protein, riboflavin, vitamin A, other nutrients.
Meats and Variety Meats; Poultry; Fish and Shellfish; Eggs: *Alternates are nuts, dried beans and peas although these are less complete protein sources.*	Two or more servings daily of 2 to 3 ounces all edible—without fat or bones—of meat, poultry or fish or 2 eggs.	Essential proteins to build, repair and regulate formation of all body tissues—muscles, organs, blood, skin and hair.
Vegetables and Fruits: *Choose those especially rich in vitamin A and vitamin C.*	Four or more servings including: One serving of a good source of vitamin C (citrus fruits, berries) or two servings of a fair source (tomatoes, cabbage). One serving at least every other day of a good source of vitamin A (deep green or yellow vegetables). A serving is ½ cup cooked vegetable or fruit or an ordinary portion	Major sources of vitamins and minerals, particularly vitamin C for healthy tissues such as gums and muscles, and vitamin A for growth, normal vision, healthy skin.

	Recommended Daily Amounts	Major Contribution
	– 1 apple, banana or orange, or half a grapefruit.	
Breads and Cereals: *Whole grain, enriched or restored breads and cereals are recommended. Alternates are pastas, rice.*	Four or more servings each day, including one serving of cereal (or five servings if no cereal is included). A serving consists of 1 slice of bread or 6 ounces ready-to-eat cereal; or ½ to ¾ cup cooked cereal, pasta or rice.	Good source of B vitamins, iron and protein; help release energy from foods, regulate appetite. Promote healthy skin and digestive tract, healthy nerves.

Dieting

A gain in weight means that more food is being eaten than the body is using up as energy each day. Food is measured in terms of its energy value by calories. Each gain of one pound in weight means that approximately 3,500 calories have been eaten in excess of the body's needs, and the excess has been stored as fat. To lose a pound it is necessary to cut calories below the body's needs in order to use up the stored excess. It is best to plan on losing weight gradually. Many different special reducing diets have been suggested as temporary ways to lose weight. None of these work over a long period of time unless habits of eating are altered, first to lose weight, and then to maintain it at a sound level. *Special reducing diets should be undertaken only after consultation with a physician.* However, it is possible for anyone to eat the basic foods indicated as daily requirements and to maintain good health with as few as 1200 calories a day, which is low enough in most cases for a regular, gradual weight loss. The amounts of proteins, vitamins, and minerals needed daily should be maintained while calories are reduced. This is best done through a diet which includes lean meats, poultry, fish or eggs, fruits and vegetables, and skim milk or low calorie cheeses.

Calories Count

The calorie values on the chart which follows are averages. They represent the most accurate generalization possible, according to government and other authoritative nutrition sources. The calorie count of foods may be determined by calculating the calories in the basic components. These consist of proteins and carbohydrates, generally calculated at 4 calories per gram, and fats, calculated at 9 calories per gram. Calories of wines or liquors are calculated on the basis of alcoholic content (½ the proof equals the percentage of alcohol) at 7 calories per gram. There are 28.3 grams to an ounce.

Calorie Counter	*Serving*	*Calories*
ALCOHOLIC BEVERAGES		
Beer	12 oz.	144
Bourbon	1½ oz.	120
Brandy	1 oz.	75
Champagne	3½ oz.	90
Cider	6 oz.	71
Cordials:		
Anisette	1 cordial glass	74
Apricot brandy	"	64
Benedictine	"	69
Creme de Menthe	"	67
Curacao	"	54
Daiquiri cocktail	4 oz.	125
Gin	1½ oz.	107
High Ball	8 oz.	150
Manhattan cocktail	4 oz.	167
Martini cocktail	4 oz.	145

Calorie Counter	Serving	Calories
Mint Julep	10 oz.	212
Old Fashioned cocktail	4 oz.	185
Planters' Punch	8 oz.	175
Rum	$1\frac{1}{2}$ oz.	105
Rye whiskey	$1\frac{1}{2}$ oz.	120
Scotch whiskey	$1\frac{1}{2}$ oz.	105
Tom Collins	10 oz.	180
Vermouth:		
French	$3\frac{1}{2}$ oz.	105
Italian	$3\frac{1}{2}$ oz.	167

BREADS

Date Nut	1 slice	100
French	"	60
Italian	"	60
Pumpernickel	"	60
Raisin	"	60
Rye	"	55
White	"	60
Whole Wheat	"	55
Muffins:		
Blueberry	1 average	112
Bran	"	130
Corn	"	150
English	"	145
Whole Wheat	"	103
Rolls:		
Hamburger	"	89
Hard	"	160
Parker House	"	115
Crackers:		
Graham	$1-2\frac{1}{2}"$ in diameter	14
Salted	$1-2"$ "	17
Soda	$1-2\frac{1}{2}"$ "	25
Matzoh	$1-6"$ "	78
Oyster	10 pieces	30
Ritz	1 piece	17
Rye Wafers	4 pieces	90

CANDIES, DESSERTS & SWEETS

Apples baked, 2 table-spoons sugar	medium	200

Calorie Counter	Serving	Calories
Apple pie	1/6 of 9" pie	400
Applesauce with sugar	1/2 cup	115
Applesauce, unsweetened	1/2 cup	50
Blueberry pie	1/6 of 9" pie	370
Brown Betty	1/2 cup	172
Cake, angel food	3" slice	165
Cake, butter with frosting	2" slice	370
Cake, chocolate with frosting	2" slice	445
Cake, sponge	2" slice	120
Candied fruits:		
Apricots	1 average	101
Cherries	1 large, 2 small	17
Citron	1" square	89
Figs	1 piece	90
Ginger Root	1 piece	17
Grapefruit, lemon, orange peel	1 tbsp. grated	32
Pineapple	1 slice	120
Caramel candy	1 oz.	115
Cherry pie	1/6 of 9" pie	414
Chocolate eclair	1 average	320
Chocolate fudge	1" square	115
Chocolate pie	1/6 of 9" pie	300
Custard	1/2 cup	142
Custard pie	1/6 of 9" pie	325
Doughnut, baking powder	1 average	125
Doughnut, yeast	1 average	130
Flavored gelatin	1/2 cup	70
Gingerbread	2" cube	175
Gumdrops	1 large, 8 small	33
Hard candy	2 sq., 2 rolls	38
Honey	1 tablespoon	65
Ice cream, chocolate	1/2 cup	180
Ice cream, vanilla	1/2 cup	145
Jam or Jelly	1 tablespoon	55
Jelly Beans	10 pieces	66
Lemon Meringue pie	1/6 of 9" pie	356
Maple syrup	1 tablespoon	55
Marmalade	1 tablespoon	55
Marshmallow	1 oz.	90
Mince pie	1/6 of 9" pie	340

Calorie Counter	Serving	Calories
Molasses	1 tablespoon	50
Pumpkin pie	1/6 of 9" pie	260
Sherbet, orange	1/6 quart	152
Sugar:		
brown	1 tablespoon	45
confectioners	1 tablespoon	30
granulated	1 tablespoon	45

CEREALS

Hot

Farina	1 cup	140
Cream of Wheat	1 cup	130
Oatmeal	1 cup	148
Rice	1 cup	164
Wheat Germ	1 cup	245
Wild Rice	1/4 cup	99

Ready to Serve

Corn flakes	1 oz.	110
Bran cereal	1/2 cup	60
Raisin bran	1/2 cup	73
Puffed rice or wheat	1 cup	55
Shredded wheat	1 large biscuit	100

DAIRY PRODUCTS

Butter or margarine	1 pat	50
Butter or margarine	1 tablespoon	100
Buttermilk	1 cup	90
Cheese:		
Blue cheese	1 tablespoon	49
Blue mold	1 oz.	103
Brick	1 oz.	103
Camembert, domestic	1 oz.	84
Cheddar, American	1 oz. 1" cube	112
Cottage	1/2 cup	120
Cream	1 oz.	105
Edam	1 oz.	87
Gruyere	1 oz.	115
Parmesan	1 oz.	110
Roquefort	1 oz.	111
Swiss	1 oz.	105
Chocolate drink milk	1 cup	190

Calorie Counter	Serving	Calories
Cream:		
Coffee	2 tablespoons	60
Heavy	2 tablespoons	110
Half & Half	2 tablespoons	40
Sour	2 tablespoons	110
Egg, boiled	1 medium	80
Egg, fried with 1 tsp. fat	1 medium	113
Egg, scrambled	1 medium	110
Milk, skim	1 cup	90
Milk, whole fresh	1 cup	160
Yogurt, plain	1 cup	120
Blueberry	1 cup	220
Orange, strawberry	1 cup	151
Pineapple	1 cup	216
Prune	1 cup	254
Red Raspberry	1 cup	225
Spiced Apple	1 cup	245
Vanilla	1 cup	186
FISH AND SEAFOOD		
Abalone, broiled	4 oz.	100
Clams, steamed	5 oz.	107
Cherrystone clams	6 clams	100
Codfish	4 oz.	180
Crabmeat, canned	3 oz.	85
Fillet of Sole	4 oz.	85
Fish sticks	5 sticks/4 oz.	100
Flounder, broiled	4 oz.	70
Haddock, broiled	4 oz.	135
Halibut, broiled	4 oz.	200
Herring	4 oz.	200
Lobster tails	4 oz.	100
Lobster, broiled	½ avg.	125
Lox, smoked	4 oz.	240
Mackerel, canned	4 oz.	205
Oyster cocktail	10 raw med.	80
Perch, broiled	4 oz.	130
Pike	4 oz.	90
Pompano, broiled	4 oz.	185
Red Snapper	4 oz.	100
Salmon, canned pink	4 oz.	160
Sardines, canned in oil	4 oz.	233

Calorie Counter	Serving	Calories
Scallops, broiled	1 svg.	140
Sea Bass	4 oz.	105
Shrimp, canned	4 oz.	125
Swordfish, broiled	4 oz.	200
Tuna, canned in oil	4 oz.	227
White Fish, baked	4 oz.	210
FRUITS & FRUIT JUICES		
Apple	medium	70
Apple juice	1 cup	120
Apricots, canned, sweetened	4 halves w/juice	105
Apricots, dried	4	39
Apricots, fresh	3 medium	55
Avocado	½ medium	185
Banana	1 medium	85
Blackberries	1 cup	85
Blueberries	1 cup	85
Boysenberries, canned	3½ oz.	38
Cantaloupe	½ of 5" melon	60
Cherries, canned	½ cup	115
Cherries, fresh	1 cup	40
Cranberry sauce	2 tablespoons	85
Dates	3 or 4	85
Figs, dried	1 large	60
Figs, fresh	3 small	90
Fruit cocktail, canned	½ cup	97
Grapefruit	½ medium	55
Grapefruit juice, canned	½ cup	95
Grape juice	1 cup	165
Grapes, green, seedless	1 cup	95
Guava	3½ oz.	62
Guava juice	4 oz.	86
Honeydew melon	¼ medium	35
Lemon	1 medium	20
Mangoes	½ medium	66
Nectarine	1 average	40
Orange	1 medium	75
Orange juice	1 cup	110
Peaches, canned	2 halves w/juice	90
Peaches, fresh	1 large	50
Pears, canned	2 halves w/juice	90

Calorie Counter	Serving	Calories
Pears, fresh	1 medium	100
Persimmons, Japanese, raw	3½ oz.	77
Persimmons, Native, raw	3½ oz.	127
Pineapple, canned	1 slice w/juice	90
Pineapple, fresh	1 cup, diced	75
Plum	1 medium	25
Prune juice	1 cup	200
Prunes, dried	1 large	17
Prunes, stewed	4 medium w/juice	75
Raisins, seedless	¼ cup	115
Raspberries, fresh	½ cup	35
Rhubarb, stewed	½ cup	192
Strawberries, fresh	1 cup	55
Strawberries, frozen	½ cup	124
Tangerine	1 average	40
Tomato	3½ oz.	22
Tomato juice	½ cup	24
Watermelon	1 slice (4″ × 8″)	115

MEATS

Bacon	1 6″ strip	50
Beef, corned	3 oz.	185
Beef, corned, hash	3 oz.	155
Beef, filet mignon	4 oz.	400
Beef, hamburger	4 oz.	325
Beef, rib roast	3 oz.	375
Beef, sirloin	3 oz.	330
Beef, tongue	3 oz.	210
Bologna	1 slice	66
Frankfurters	1 average	155
Ham, baked	3 oz.	245
Ham, boiled	3 oz.	201
Lamb, roast leg	3 oz.	235
Lamb chop, broiled	4 oz.	400
Liver, beef	2 oz.	130
Liver, calf	1 slice (3″ × 2¼″ × ⅜″)	74
Pork chop	3½ oz.	260
Pork roast	2 slices	310
Veal chop, loin	3 oz.	185
Veal roast	3 oz.	230
Veal cutlet	3½ oz.	277

Calorie Counter	Serving	Calories
POULTRY		
Chicken, fried	drumstick	90
Chicken, broiled	3 oz.	115
Chicken, fried	½ breast	155
Duck, roasted	1 slice (3½" × 2½" × ¼")	109
Squab, flesh only	3½ oz.	142
Turkey, roasted	2 slices (4½" × 2½" × ¼")	190
NUTS & NIBBLES		
Almonds	12–15 nuts	90
Brazil nuts	¼ cup	229
Cashew nuts	¼ cup	190
Chestnuts, fresh	2 large	29
Chestnuts, dried	1 cup	377
Chestnuts, shelled	½ cup	191
Coconut, dried	2 tablespoons	42
Filberts or Hazelnuts	10–12 nuts	97
Hickory nuts	15 small nuts	101
Macadamia nuts, roasted	6 whole	109
Peanuts	¼ cup halves	210
Pecans	¼ cup halves	185
Pistachio nuts	30 nuts	88
Walnuts	¼ cup halves	162
Cheese tidbits, crackers	15 crackers	81
Corn chips	1 serving	292
Popcorn, plain	1 cup	54
Potato chips	1 piece	13
Pretzels	3½ oz.	390
PASTA		
Macaroni, cooked firm	1 cup	207
Noodles, egg	1 cup	200
Pizza with cheese	3½ oz.	236
Spaghetti, cooked firm	1 cup	216
SOUPS		
Asparagus, cream of, canned	1 cup	110
Celery, cream of, canned	1 cup	122
Chicken noodle	1 cup	65
Clam chowder, Manhattan	1 cup	87

Calorie Counter	Serving	Calories
Mushroom, cream of	1 cup	120
Minestone	1/3 can	72
Onion	1/3 can	37
Pea soup	1 cup	130
Tomato soup, cream of	1 cup	125
Vegetable (beef base)	1 cup	80

VEGETABLES

Artichokes	1 medium	45
Asparagus	8 stalks	25
Beans, green	1/2 cup	15
Beets	1/2 cup	25
Broccoli	2/3 cup or 1 lg. stalk	26
Brussels sprouts	6 or 1/2 cup	22
Cabbage	1/2 cup, chopped	12
Cabbage, cooked	1/2 cup	15
Carrots	1 medium, raw	20
Carrots, cooked	1/2 cup	22
Cauliflower	1 cup	25
Celery	2 medium stalks	10
Coleslaw	1 cup	120
Corn, fresh	1 medium ear	70
Cucumber	1/2 medium	15
Green pepper	1 medium	15
Kale, cooked	1 cup	30
Lettuce	1/4 large head	15
Lima beans	1/2 cup	90
Mushrooms, canned	1/2 cup	20
Mushrooms, fresh	10 small	15
Okra	10 pods	30
Onion	1 2 1/2" diameter	40
Parsnips	1 cup	100
Peas, canned	1/2 cup	82
Peas, fresh cooked	1/2 cup	55
Potato, baked	1 average	90
Potato, boiled	1 average	90
Potato, sweet, baked	1 average	155
Potato, french fried	10 pieces	155
Radish	1 medium	1
Sauerkraut	1 cup	45
Spinach, cooked	1/2 cup	20
Squash, summer, cooked	1/2 cup	15

Calorie Counter	Serving	Calories
Squash, winter, cooked	½ cup	65
Turnip greens, cooked	1 cup	25
Watercress	1 bunch	10
Yams	½ cup	105
Zucchini, cooked	1 cup	30

Food Shopping

Efficient Marketing. It pays to develop special skills in shopping for food. You'll get the best value for your money and the best possible meals for yourself. Food markets offer a great selection of foodstuffs and a wide variety of forms in which foods may be purchased.

Five simple rules are basic for efficient marketing:

1. Plan meals in advance—if possible, a week ahead, and buy with your advance needs in mind.
2. Keep the menus flexible enough to allow you to take advantage of special prices at the market.
3. Take advantage of plentiful seasonal foods in planning menus.
4. Keep your basic food supplies stocked, checking refrigerator, vegetable bin, cupboards and freezer before you begin to shop. See that the makings of an emergency meal and impromptu snack are on hand.
5. Read the labels of foods you select. You will find ingredients of the contents listed in order of importance, along with description of the product and information on use.

When you shop, select your purchases in this order: canned goods, package goods, household supplies and other imperishables first; then dairy products, meat, fresh fruits and vegetables, and frozen foods last, so that they will have the shortest possible wait before they reach their destination.

Storing Food. As soon as you arrive home, unpack your purchases, sorting into groups: frozen foods to go directly into the freezer; meats and poultry to be unwrapped, then covered loosely for storage in refrigerator or re-wrapped for freezing; fruits and vegetables, separating those for refrigeration and those to be stored elsewhere; dairy products, assembled so that they may be carried easily to refrigerator and stored; packaged goods grouped for storage in respective cupboards.

Work with items which require freezing or refrigeration first. Remember that foods tend to lose moisture or take on other flavors in the refrigerator. Wrap foods for storage in plastic bags or wrappings, or store in tightly covered plastic or glass containers; store vegetables in a closed container or the crisper drawer.

The temperature of the refrigerator should be between 38° and 42° F. An accumulation of frost on the freezing coils can raise the temperature dangerously. Defrost refrigerator as often as necessary to prevent this, especially in warm weather or when the refrigerator is being opened frequently. (In refrigerators equipped with automatic defrosters, check drip pan as indicated in manufacturer's directions.)

Consumer Protection Tips. Below is a checklist of points for market shopping that will help you get full value for your dollar.

1. See that the store has a scale that can be easily read.
2. Get the price per pound or unit price before you buy.
3. See that the scale pointer is at zero before the merchandise is weighed and that it is at rest before a weight or price is quoted.

4. Figure the total price yourself; question any higher amount.
5. Ask to have every obstruction removed to give you a clear view of the scale or cash register.
6. Check purchases against itemized register tape and re-add the total of the tape.
7. You are entitled to net weight of your purchase, not including boxes, cartons, bags or wrapping paper.
8. Buy fresh fruits and vegetables in season; they taste better and are much lower in price.
9. Check the label on all prepackaged foods, including frozen foods, to see what is contained, the net weight, and the total price.
10. If in doubt, check weights of prepackaged items on the customers scale or ask that they be weighed in your presence.
11. Don't be fooled by the size of the container or box; look for the weight or content statement.
12. Whenever possible, buy in person. If you must order by phone, insist that itemized bills accompany your order.
13. If a reputable store has a special sale, stock up, especially on staples and canned goods.
14. If you have your meat ground to order, see that the grinding takes place in front of you.

To this list add these do's and don'ts:

DO	DON'T
► prepare a shopping list.	► shop on an empty stomach, or you may be tempted to make impulse purchases.
► look for advertised specials before you shop. Demand a raincheck if they are not in stock.	► let your market lure you into making trips

DO

- be sure the advertised price is stamped on the item.
- look for the date stamped on most dairy products and baked goods.
- read the labels on all pre-packaged foods, including frozen, for net weight and ingredients.
- check the label on packaged meat, whole or chopped, for the cut it comes from, like rib, chuck, sirloin. This must be stated.

DON'T

for advertised specials that they never seem to have. Stores that advertise specials must have adequate supplies on hand.

- be charged a higher price than advertised.
- buy the closest date. Do look for the date furthest in the future — this product will stay fresher longer.
- be fooled by fancy names on packaged meat. They don't mean anything.
- forget your eyeglasses when you shop!

One last note: it is an FTC rule that supermarkets must make specials available at the price advertised — either right on the shelf or immediately upon request (Federal Trade Commission Buyers Guide No. 11). So make the best use of advertising. Take a *Special Sale* ad with you to the supermarket, or look at the newspaper ads posted at the store, and be sure you find the specials at the prices advertised.

If rainchecks get to be a habit, the FTC says you can help kick a supermarket's habit of being sold out by complaining to the manager, protesting to the manager's boss, switching to another store where specials are on hand as advertised, and by writing to your nearest FTC office. Give all the facts and a copy of the ad.

Necessities of Life: Food ◄ 49

FTC REGIONAL OFFICES & FIELD STATIONS

Atlanta, Ga.
Boston, Mass.
Buffalo, N.Y.
Charlotte, N.C.
Chicago, Ill.
Cleveland, Ohio
Dallas, Texas
Denver, Colo.
Detroit, Mich.
Honolulu, Hawaii
Kansas City, Mo.
Los Angeles, Calif.
Miami, Fla.
New Orleans, La.
New York, N.Y.
Oak Ridge, Tenn.
Philadelphia, Pa.
Phoenix, Ariz.
Portland, Ore.
St. Louis, Mo.
San Antonio, Texas
San Diego, Calif.
San Francisco, Calif.
Seattle, Wash.
Washington, D.C.

Buying Meat. When buying meat it is important to select the right cut for the cooking method you prefer, keeping in mind that the edible portions of the cheapest cut are as high in nutritional value and as good to eat, when properly prepared, as the most expensive cut.

Meat may be cooked in dry heat (roasted, baked, broiled) or in a moist heat (pot roast, stews). Thin cuts of tender meat may be cooked in a small amount of fat, a process called pan-frying or sautéing. In deep-frying the meat is cooked quickly in fat deep enough to cover it completely.

OVEN TEMPERATURES

	Degrees Fahrenheit	*Degrees Celsius*[*] *(approx. equiv.)*
Very Slow	250°	120°
Slow	300°	150°
Moderately Slow	325°	165°
Moderate	350°	175°
Moderately Hot	375°	190°
Hot	400°	205°
Very Hot	450°	230°
Extremely Hot	500°	260°

[*] Celsius measurements have been included throughout due to the expected changeover to the metric measuring system in the United States.

To cook frozen meat roasts *without* defrosting, increase the cooking time by one-third to one-half. The extra time needed to cook frozen steaks, chops, and hamburgers depends upon the thickness and size of the meat.

Beef Standards. There are two standards by which beef can be judged: the packer's own brand and the U.S.

ROASTING CHART FOR BEEF CUTS

Insert meat thermometer into thickest part of meat away from fat and bone. Use shorter time per pound for larger cuts, and longer time for smaller cuts. Carving will be easier if meat is removed from oven 20 to 30 minutes before serving.

Beef Cut	Weight	Oven Temperatures	Meat Thermometer Reading	Cooking Time Minutes Per Pound
Standing Rib	4–8 pounds	325° F or 165° C	140 (rare) 160 (medium) 170 (well-done)	18–20 22–25 27–30
Rolled Rib	4–6 pounds	325° F or 165° C	140 (rare) 160 (medium) 170 (well-done)	28–30 32–35 37–40
Rolled Rump	4–6 pounds	325° F or 165° C	140 (rare) 160 (medium)	25–30 32–35
Rib Eye	4–6 pounds	325° F or 165° C	140 (rare) 160 (medium) 170 (well-done)	18–20 20–22 22–25
Sirloin Tip	3–5 pounds	325° F or 165° C	140 (rare) 160 (medium)	30 35
Whole Fillet	4–5 pounds	425° F or 220° C	140 (rare)	10

Department of Agriculture grade. Beef stamped *Prime* by the USDA is principally sold to restaurants and hotels, but you'll find an occasional butcher who sells it, too. The next two grades are *Choice* and *Good* and are generally available at retail markets. *Good* has the least fat, is somewhat less juicy and tender, and is the least expensive of the grades.

Veal. Veal is the meat of the calf. It is most popular in France, Austria, and particularly in Italy where people feel it tastes better than beef. Tender, delicate veal comes from a milk-fed animal no more than 14 weeks old. If it is older, cooking takes longer and extra seasoning is needed to give it flavor.

Leg of veal is considered by many to be the choicest cut. It is from the leg that we get scallopine of veal (veal scallops) and veal cutlets. Shoulder and breast of veal are more economical and can be made into delicious entrées especially when stuffed and braised.

Don't rush veal. Cook it slowly and always serve well-done.

VEAL ROASTING CHART

Oven temperature is 325° F (165° Celsius) for all cuts.

Cut of Veal	Weight	Meat Thermometer Reading	Cooking Time Minutes Per Pound
Leg	5–8 lbs.	170–180° F or 77–82° C	35
Loin	4–6 lbs.	170–180° F or 77–82° C	35–40
Rolled Shoulder Stuffed	3–5 lbs.	170–180° F or 77–82° C	40–45
Breast			40–45
Shoulder	4–6 lbs.	170–180° F or 77–82° C	35–40

Lamb and Mutton. Lamb is the meat of the sheep under one year of age. Mutton comes from sheep over one

BEEF

CHUCK
- Inside Chuck Roll
- Chuck Short Ribs
- Chuck Tender
- Petite Steaks
- Blade Pot Roast
- Arm Pot Roast
- Boneless Shoulder Pot Roast
- English (Boston) Cut

RIB
- Standing Rib Roast
- Rib Steak
- Rib Steak, Boneless
- Delmonico Roast
- Delmonico Steak

SHORT LOIN
- Club Steak
- T-Bone Steak
- Porterhouse Steak
- Top Loin Steak
- Filet Mignon

SIRLOIN
- Pin Bone Sirloin Steak
- Flat Bone Sirloin Steak
- Wedge Bone Sirloin Steak
- Boneless Sirloin Steak

ROUND
- Standing Rump
- Rolled Rump
- Round Steak
- Top Round Steak
- Outside Bottom Round Roast
- Outside Bottom Round Steak
- Heel of Round
- Eye of Round

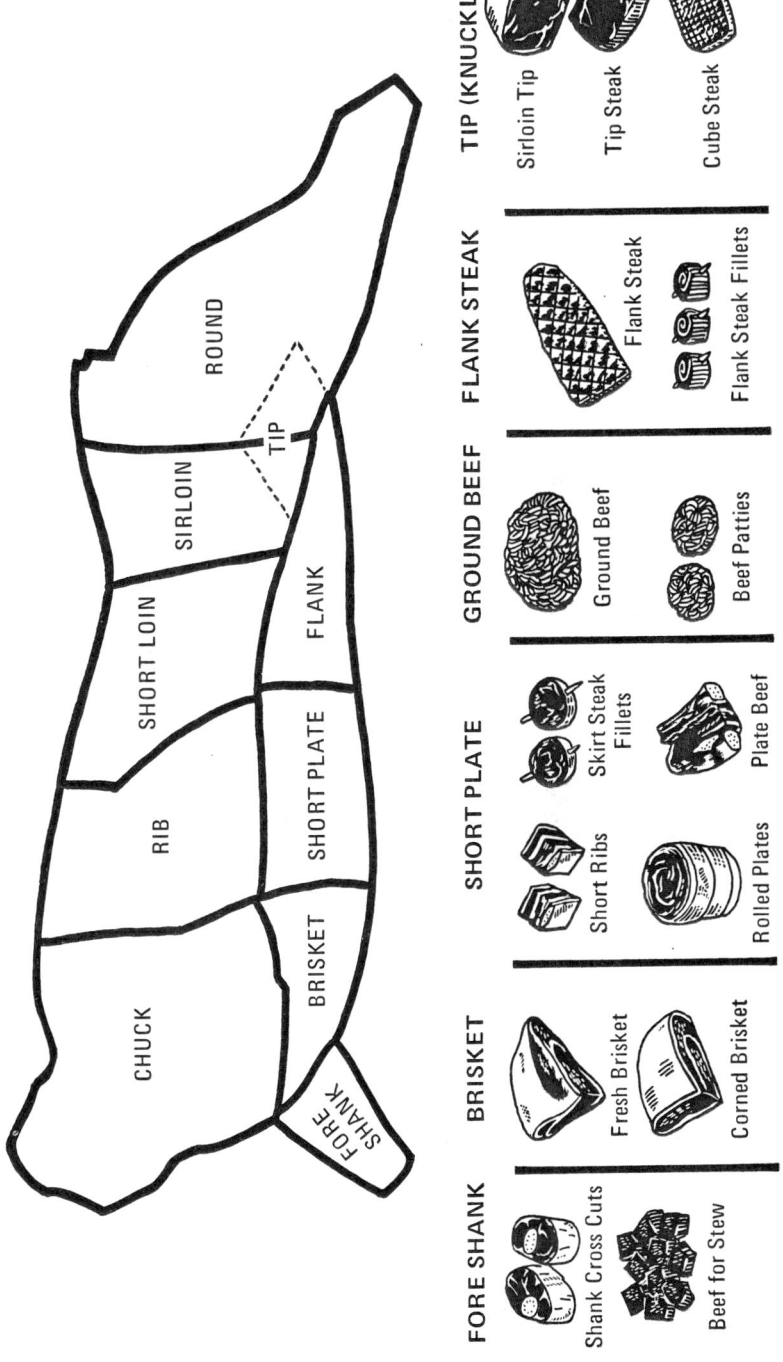

VEAL

SHOULDER

Blade Roast

Arm Roast

Rolled Shoulder

Blade Steak

Arm Steak

Neck

Veal for Stew

RACK

Rib Roast

Crown Roast

Rib Chop

Trenched Rib Chop

LOIN

Loin Roast

Rolled Stuffed Loin

Loin Chop

Kidney Chop

SIRLOIN

Sirloin Roast

Rolled Double Sirloin

Sirloin Steak

Cube Steak

LEG

Standing Rump

Shank Half of Leg

Center Leg

Rolled Leg

Heel of Round

Round Steak

Cutlets—Boneless

Rolled Cutlets (Birds)

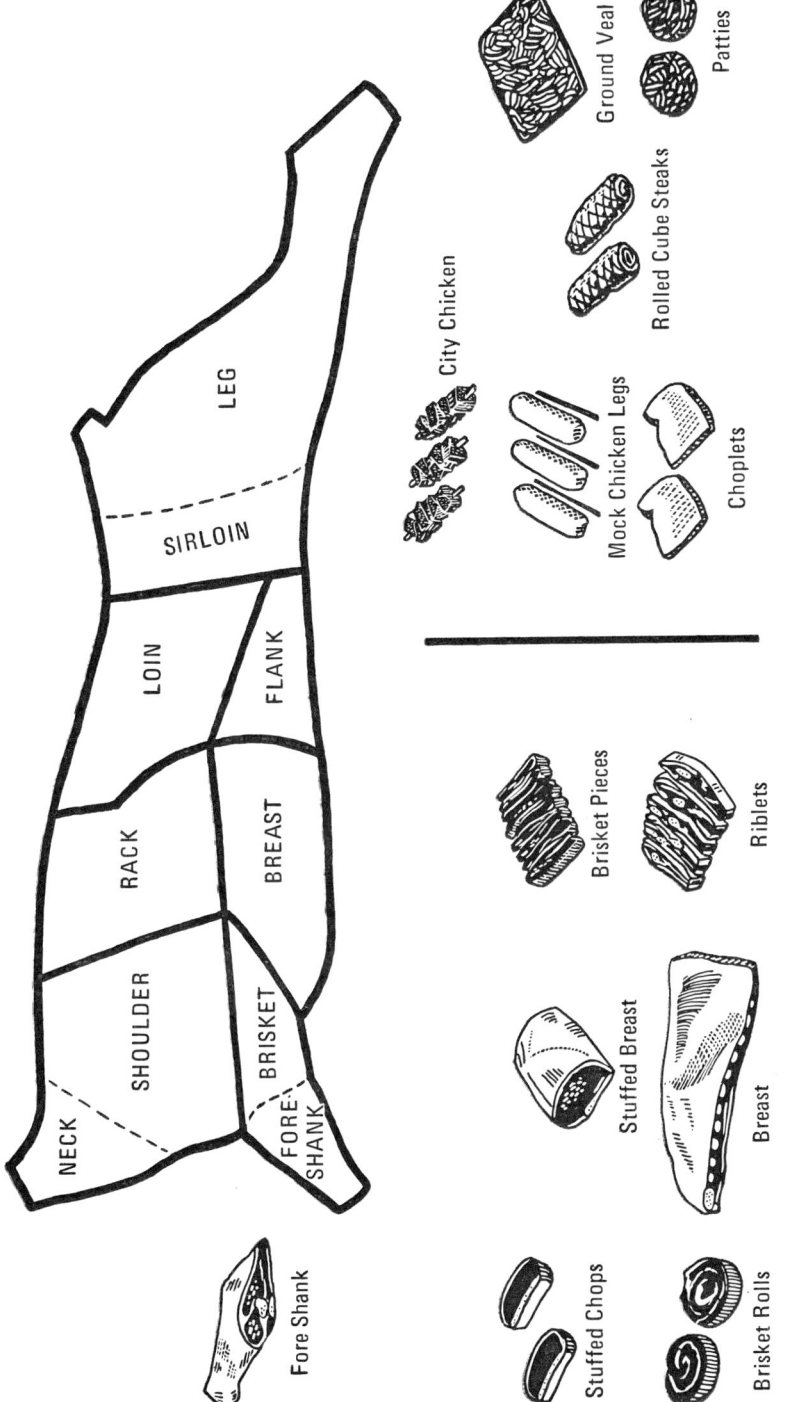

LAMB

SHOULDER

- Square Shoulder
- Rolled Shoulder
- Cushion Shoulder
- Cubes for Shish Kabobs

RACK

- Rib Roast
- Crown Roast
- Rib Chops
- Frenched Rib Chops

LOIN

- Loin Roast
- Rolled Double Loin
- English Chops
- Loin Chops

SIRLOIN

- Sirloin Roast
- Rolled Double Sirloin
- Sirloin Chop

LEG

- Leg Sirloin On
- Sirloin Half of Leg
- Shank Half of Leg
- Leg - Sirloin Off
- Leg Chop
- American Leg
- Rolled Leg
- Center Leg
- Combination Leg

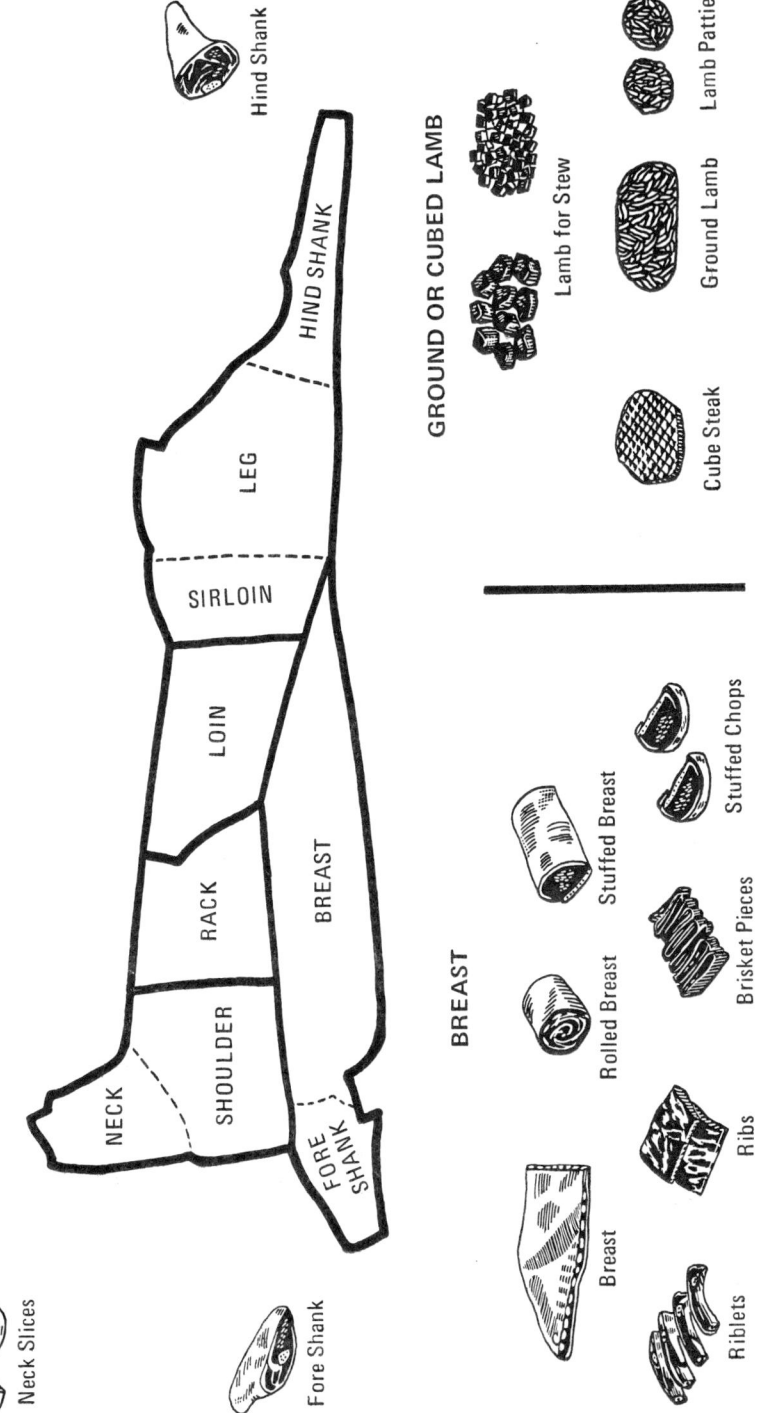

PORK

LEG (HAM)

Smoked Ham, Butt Portion

Canned Ham

Smoked Ham Boneless Roll

Smoked Ham Center Slice

Smoked Ham Shank Portion

Rolled Fresh Ham

Sliced Cooked Boiled Ham

LOIN

Smoked Loin Chop

Tenderloin

Country Style Backbone

Back Ribs

Canadian Style Bacon

Blade Loin Roast

Sirloin Roast

Sirloin Chop

Top Loin Chop

Rolled Loin Roast

Center Loin Roast

Loin Chop

Butterfly Chop

Rib Chop

Blade Chop

SHOULDER BUTT

Smoked Shoulder Butt

Rolled Boston Butt

Boston Butt

Sausage

Blade Steak

Porklet

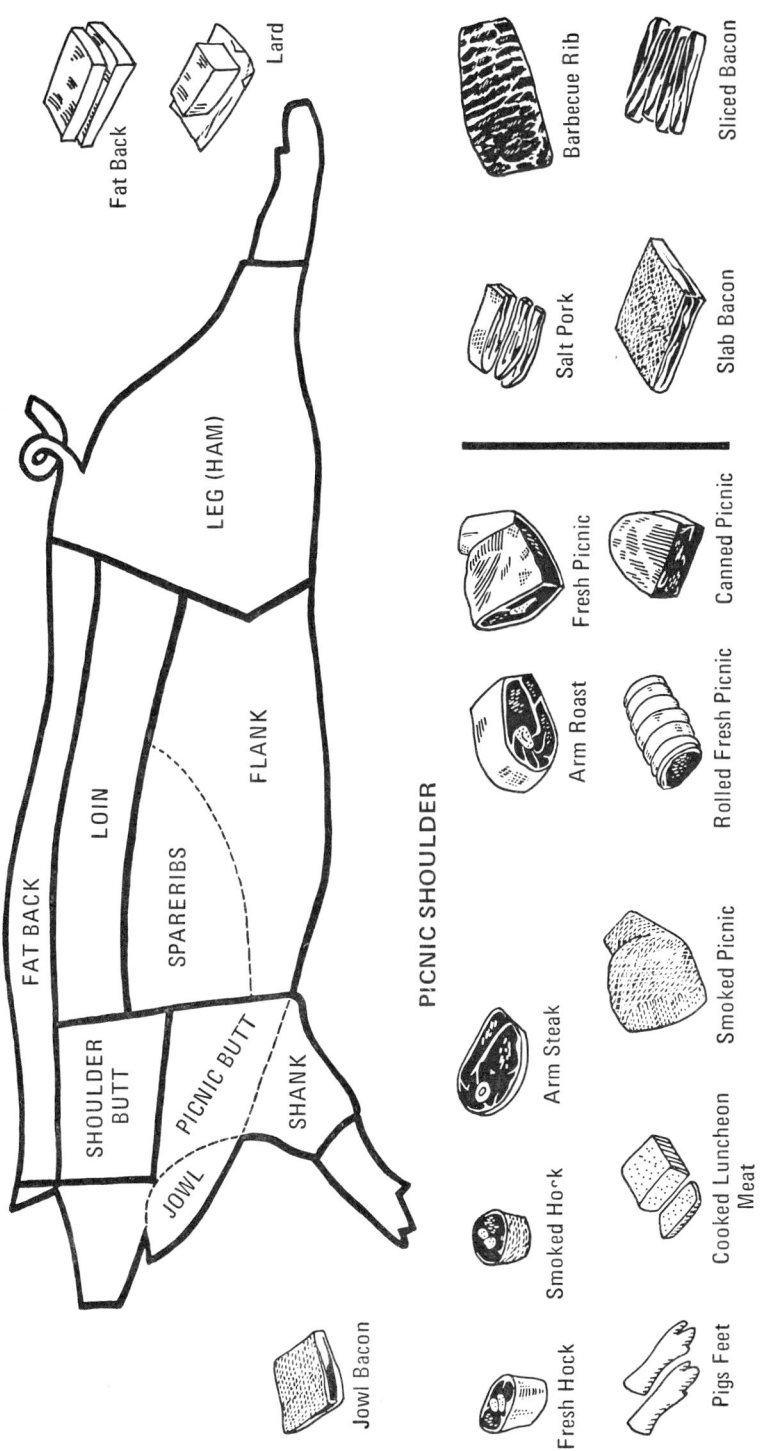

year of age, has a stronger flavor than lamb, and is less popular but also less expensive.

Lamb is graded like beef—Prime, Choice, Good. Prime is the finest quality, but Choice is also excellent. Roasting cuts are the leg, the shoulder, and the rack. Until recently, Americans tended to overcook lamb. The fact is, it's better when served pink or rare.

LAMB ROASTING CHART

Oven temperature is 325° F (165° Celsius) for all cuts.

Cut of Lamb	Weight	Meat Thermometer Reading	Cooking Time Minutes Per Pound
Leg	5-8 lbs.	165-170 °F (rare) or 75-77 °C	25-30
		175-180° F (medium) or 80-82 °C	30-35
Shoulder (cushion)	3-5 lbs.	175-180 °F or 80-82 °C	30-35
Rolled Shoulder	3-5 lbs.	175-180 °F or 80-82 °C	35-45
Crown Roast	4-6 lbs.	175-180 °F or 80-82 °C	35-45

LAMB BROILING CHART

	Thickness	Medium	Well-Done
Lamb Chops	3/4″	5 minutes°	6-7 minutes°
Rib, Loin, Shoulder	1½″	9 minutes°	11 minutes°

° Time per side.

Mutton is cooked like lamb, and cooking times above apply also to mutton chops and roasts.

Pork. Every part of the pig is edible but it must be cooked thoroughly. Meat should always achieve a thermometer reading of 160°-185° F (72-85° C).

The loin is the most popular roast of pork. Shoulder of pork also roasts well.

There are three types of pork chops: loin, rib, and shoulder. Loin is the choicest.

Pork steak and fresh ham come from the leg. Spareribs are delicious when barbecued.

Allow one pound per person for most pork cuts because bone and fat take up part of the weight.

PORK ROASTING CHART

Oven temperature is 325° F (165° Celsius) for all cuts.

	Weight	Meat Thermometer Reading	Cooking Time Minutes Per Pound
Loin	2–7 lbs.	185° F or 85° C	35–45
Boston Butt (shoulder)	4–6 lbs.	185° F or 85° C	45–50
Cushion Shoulder	5 lbs.	185° F or 85° C	40–45
Leg (Fresh Ham)	5–6 lbs.	185° F or 85° C	40–50
Crown Roast	6–7 lbs.	185° F or 85° C	45–50

HAM BAKING CHART

Oven temperature is 325° F (165° Celsius) for all cuts. (Follow package directions or the following chart.)

Cut of Ham	Weight	Meat Thermometer Reading	Cooking Time Minutes Per Pound
For Uncooked Smoked Hams			
Whole Ham (Bone in)	8–20 lbs.	160° F or 72° C	18–20
Whole Ham (Boned)	8–16 lbs.	160° F or 72° C	18–20

HAM BAKING CHART (*Continued*)

Cut of Ham	Weight	Meat Thermometer Reading	Cooking Time Minutes Per Pound
Shank Half Ham or Butt Portion (Bone in)	4–8 lbs.	160° F or 72° C	35–40
Picnic (Bone in)	4–10 lbs.	170° F or 77° C	35–40
For Pre-Cooked Hams — To Heat Before Eating			
Whole Ham (Bone in)	8–20 lbs.	130° F or 55° C	15
Whole Ham (Boned)	8–16 lbs.	130° F or 55° C	˙15
Shank Half Ham or Butt Portion (Bone in)	4–8 lbs.	130° F or 55° C	15–20
Picnic (Bone in)	4–10 lbs.	130° F or 55° C	25–35
Canadian Bacon		170° F or 77° C	35–40

Carving Meats. Meat looks better and goes farther when carved correctly. Always let meat stand to set the juices before attempting to carve it — about 20 minutes in a warm place for roasts, about 5 minutes for steaks. Use a wooden carving board or heated platter large enough to easily accommodate the meat.

You should have a sharp heavy-bladed carving knife and a two-pronged carving fork. A long flexible knife for thin slices and a smaller carving knife for fowl and steaks would be useful, too.

Meat is generally carved with the grain rather than against it.

Poultry. Poultry is extremely versatile and it can be purchased in several forms. Whole, it can be roasted, boiled, braised, or cooked on the rotisserie. The split version is good for broiling or barbecuing and cut up poultry is suitable for frying and sautéing as well as for broiling or barbecuing.

Chicken and turkey are best when they're fresh-killed. Try to find a butcher shop that has daily deliveries from a farm. Next best is quick frozen poultry. Once you thaw frozen chicken or turkey you *must* use it. Don't let it stand too long and don't try to refreeze it unless it has been cooked first.

Cold storage poultry has the least flavor. When you buy poultry, allow one pound of fowl per person.

Carving Poultry. Place chicken, turkey or other fowl, breast up, on heated platter with neck to left of carver. Bend leg away from body, cut between leg and body and divide at joint. Repeat with other leg. Cut off wings in same manner. Remove legs and wings to separate heated plate. Insert carving fork alongside the breastbone. Cut the breast meat in thin slices parallel to the breastbone, beginning above the wing and working up. Place the pieces neatly on one side of the platter. Divide legs at the joint, and, if fowl is large, slice legs and second joints. Separate the collarbone from the breast, slip the knife under the shoulder blade and turn it over. Cut and separate the breast from the back.

Chicken. Chickens are plentiful and relatively inexpensive.

Broiler-fryers are only nine weeks old, weigh from $1\frac{1}{2}$ to $3\frac{1}{2}$ pounds and are usually tender and juicy. The roaster is about twelve weeks old, weighs about $3\frac{1}{2}$ to 5 pounds, costs more per pound, and takes longer to cook. The stewing hen can be $1\frac{1}{2}$ years of age, usually weighs 4 to 6 pounds and requires even longer to cook.

Capon, altered rooster, can weigh as much as 7 pounds and is considered a luxury roast.

Chicken has excellent nutritional value — high in protein and lower in calories than most meats.

CHART FOR ROASTING STUFFED CHICKEN

Class	Weight	Temperature	Cooking Time Hours
Broiler-fryer	1½–3 lbs.	375° F or 190° C	1–1½
Roaster	3½–6 lbs.	325° F or 165° C	2–3
Capon	5–7 lbs.	325° F or 165° C	2½–3½

Turkey. Once only a holiday treat, turkey is now readily available the year round in sizes from 4-pound broilers up to toms of 30 pounds and more. When you buy turkey, look for firm, fresh looking skin, plump legs and thighs, and a thick breast. Long, scrawny turkeys are not as tender or tasty.

CHART FOR ROASTING STUFFED TURKEY

Size of Bird	Open Roasting Pan Oven Temperature	Cooking Time Hours
6–8 lbs.	325 °F or 165 °C	3–3½
8–12 lbs.	325 °F or 165 °C	3½–4½
12–16 lbs.	325 °F or 165 °C	4½–5
16–20 lbs.	300 °F or 150 °C	5–6½
	Wrapped in Foil	
6–8 lbs.	450 °F or 232 °C	1½–2
8–12 lbs.	450 °F or 232 °C	2–2½
12–16 lbs.	450 °F or 232 °C	3–3½
16–20 lbs.	450 °F or 232 °C	3½–4

For unstuffed birds, reduce cooking time by 20 minutes.

Duck. Most ducks sold in this country are Long Island ducks, a strain developed recently as an all-purpose fowl. Long Island ducks, with a heavy layer of fat under their skin, require slow cooking. One duck usually will serve two people.

When roasting a duck, use a pan with a rack or spit. Fat will cook out into the dripping pan and the duck will remain crisp.

Buying and Preparing Fish. Fish is least expensive and most appealing when it is freshly caught in season (see "Seasonal Seafood Chart"). But a wide variety of fish and seafood is now deep frozen soon after the catch.

Because of its comparatively low cost, high food value and a generally low calorie count, fish should be served often.

Usually the fish that you purchase will be ready to use — cleaned and scaled, skinned, boned, or filleted. Fish markets will prepare your choice of fresh fish for the cooking method you plan to use. When using commercially frozen fish, follow directions on the package. Many of these products can be cooked in the frozen state without thawing. To thaw home-frozen fish, let it stand overnight in the refrigerator; then dry and cook at once.

SEASONAL SEAFOOD CHART

All Year Round	Bluefish	Mackerel	Whitefish
	Butterfish	Perch	Whiting
	Cod	Red Snapper	Crabmeat
	Flounder	Salmon	Lobster
	Haddock	Sole	Scallops
	Halibut	Trout	Shrimp
June 1–December 1	Bullheads		
	Catfish		
	Pickerel		
	Walleyed Pike		
April 1–June 1	Shad		
November 1–May 1	Smelts		
September 1–May 1	Oysters		
June 1–August 1	Soft-shell Crabs		

COOKING METHODS FOR SEAFOOD

Fish	Boiling	Broiling	Frying	Baking
Black Bass		x	x	x
Bluefish		x		x
Bloater		x		
Brook Trout			x	
Bullhead			x	
Butterfish			x	
Carp	x	x	x	x
Catfish			x	
Cod	x	x	x	x
Flounder		x	x	x
Haddock	x		x	x
Hake		x		x
Halibut	x	x	x	x
Herring	x		x	
Mackerel, fresh	x	x		x
Mackerel, salt	x			
Mullet				x
Muskellunge	x			
Perch			x	x
Pickerel	x		x	x
Pike	x	x	x	x
Pollock			x	
Pompono	x	x	x	
Porgy		x		
Red Snapper	x		x	x
Salmon	x	x	x	x
Sea Bass	x	x		x
Shad		x		x
Shad Roe		x	x	
Sheepshead	x			
Smelts			x	
Sole	x		x	x
Sturgeon		x		x
Tilefish	x	x		
Trout			x	x
Weakfish	x			x
Whitefish		x	x	x
Whiting		x	x	

Buying and Storing Vegetables. Buy the freshest, most perfect, unblemished vegetables possible, always in small quantities that you can use within a day or two. Packed vegetables may be refrigerated in the plastic bags in which they are sold. Potatoes and onions should be stored in a cool, airy, dry place. Sweet potatoes do not keep well so buy only what you plan to use at once. Salad greens should be washed and stored at once in refrigerator bags or in the vegetable crisper.

Cooking Vegetables. Vegetables, possibly more than any other food, require proper cooking and seasoning to bring out their maximum appeal. To preserve vitamins and minerals, pare them as thinly as possible. Don't soak vegetables except for cleaning. And don't add soda to the cooking water—it destroys vitamins. Vegetables look and taste best when they are cooked until just tender in a minimum amount of liquid. Overcooking destroys flavor, color, and texture.

Seasonings and sauces should bring out, not disguise the flavor of vegetables.

Fruits. Delightful and refreshing, fruits are used mainly as desserts or snacks. However, their position in the recipe book goes far beyond this. Fruits find their way into salads, sauces, even soups. In addition to the fruits with which you are probably most familiar—apples, bananas, apricots, peaches, pears, oranges, tangerines, cherries, berries, plums, and melons—there are many other refreshing varieties. Here are a few to consider.

> Avocados—Sometimes called alligator pears. Tremendous in salads and made into a sauce for salads or dips.
>
> Dates—Fruit with a nutty taste. Some people prefer dates with sweet cream. Great in cookies and quick breads.

Figs — Fine alone or in wine.

Guava — A tropical delicacy. Delightful in sauce or as a spread.

Honeydew — This pale green melon is good, when ripe, as an appetizer with a piece of prosciutto ham or for dessert.

Litchis — Commonly found in Chinese restaurants, they're a connoisseur's delight.

Mangoe — This intriguing tropical fruit is delicious ripe; serve by itself or in brandied syrup.

Nectarine — The peach without the fuzz; usually smaller than a peach but just as tasty and refreshing.

Oriental Persimmon — This fruit has bright orange skins and must be eaten absolutely ripe, as the skins melt into the flesh of the fruit.

Papaya — An exotic fruit, the papaya is a melon that grows on a tree and is bright pink. Try it garnished with cherries.

Pomegrante — This red fruit is succulent when ripe. Its name means apple of many seeds. Juice is used to make grenadine.

Pumpkin — Pumpkin is for pies and soup; the seeds are great when dried, roasted, and salted.

Prunes — Serve alone dry or stewed or add these to the apricots and almonds soaking in brandy. A good source of iron.

Cheese. Cheese is an indispensible dairy product. Rich in protein, it's not only a quick snack and a good accompaniment for apple pie, it often forms the base for many casseroles and sauces. Cheese can be classified as ripened or unripened. Cottage cheese, ricotta, and cream cheese are all unripened cheeses in contrast to ripened cheeses which have been allowed to age under set conditions to develop flavor and texture. The cheese chart which follows will serve as a guide for your first journeys into the world of cheeses. You're sure to find several that suit your taste. There are many more than those listed here.

CHEESE
Soft, Ripened and Unripened

Name	Origin	Type	Flavor	Texture	Color	Usage
Cottage, plain or creamed	Unknown	Unripened	Mild	Soft, curd particles of varying size	White	Salads, with fruits, baked dishes, dips, sandwiches
Cream	United States	Unripened	Mild	Soft and smooth	White	Salads, dips, sandwiches, spread, cake topping; useful in cooking
Neufchatel	France	Unripened	Mild	Soft and smooth; similar to cream cheese but with a lower fat content	White	Salads, dips, sandwiches; popular dessert cheese
Ricotta	Italy	Unripened	Mild	Soft, moist like cottage cheese or dry, suitable for grating	White	Usually used in cooking
Brie	France	Ripened	Mild to pungent; distinctive taste	Soft and smooth	Creamy yellow inside; thin brown and white crust	Appetizers, with crackers and fruit, dessert

Name	Origin	Type	Flavor	Texture	Color	Usage
Camembert	France	Ripened	Mild to pungent	Soft, almost runny	Creamy yellow inside; white crust	Appetizers with crackers and fruit, dessert
Limburger	Germany	Ripened	Strong	Soft and smooth with small irregular openings	Creamy yellow inside; reddish yellow surface	Appetizers, desserts, with crackers, rye or other dark breads
Semisoft, Ripened and Unripened						
Bel Paese	Italy	Ripened	Sharp	Creamy with a firm rind; soft to medium firm	Creamy yellow inside; grayish or brownish surface	Appetizers, desserts, with crackers, in sandwiches
Brick	United States	Ripened	Mild to sharp	Semisoft to medium firm; elastic with small holes	Creamy yellow	Appetizers, desserts, in sandwiches
Edam	Netherlands	Ripened	Mild, salty	Semisoft to firm, smooth	Creamy yellow or medium	Appetizers, desserts, spread for crackers

Gouda	Netherlands	Ripened	Similar to Edam	Semisoft to firm	Creamy yellow or medium yellow-orange; rind is usually but not always red	Appetizers, desserts, in sandwiches
Muenster	Germany	Ripened	Pungent	Semisoft to hard	Creamy white inside; yellow-tan surface	Appetizers, desserts, in sandwiches
Mozzarella	Italy	Unripened	Delicate	Slightly firm, plastic	Creamy white	May be eaten sliced or used in baking dishes
Port du Salut	France	Ripened	Mellow	Semisoft, smooth	Creamy yellow inside; brownish crust	Appetizers, desserts, good with fruit in fondues

Firm, Ripened and Unripened

Name	Origin	Type	Flavor	Texture	Color	Usage
Caciocavallo	Italy	Ripened	Piquant	Firm	Light or white inside; clay or tan-colored surface	Desserts, snacks, can be grated if fully cured and dried
Cheddar	England	Ripened	Mild to very sharp	Firm and smooth	White to medium yellow-orange	Appetizers, desserts, in sandwiches, cooked dishes
Parmesan	Italy	Ripened	Sharp	Very hard, granular	Creamy white	Used as seasoning
Provolone	Italy	Ripened	Mellow to sharp, smoky	Firm and smooth	Light creamy inside; light brown or golden yellow surface	Appetizers, desserts and snacks
Romano	Italy	Ripened	Sharp	Very hard, granular	Yellow-white inside; greenish black crust	Grated for seasoning

Sapsago	Switzerland	Ripened	Sharp	Very hard	Light green	Grated for seasoning
Swiss	Switzerland	Ripened	Mild, nut-like	Firm, smooth with large eyes (gas holes)	Light yellow, almost white	Favorite for sandwiches; fondues
Blue Vein Mold						
Blue or Bleu	United States	Ripened	Sharp, salty	Semisoft to hard, sometimes crumbly	White inside, marbled with blue veins of mold	Appetizers, desserts, dips, salad dressing, sandwich spreads
Gorgonzola	Italy	Ripened	Similar to Blue	Semisoft sometimes crumbly	Creamy white inside streaked with blue-green veins of mold; clay-colored surface	Same as Blue
Roquefort	France	Ripened	Sharp, slightly peppery	Semisoft, sometimes crumbly	White or creamy white inside, marbled with	Same as Blue

▶ 73

Name	Origin	Type	Flavor	Texture	Color	Usage
Stilton	England	Ripened	Piquant, milder than Roquefort	Semisoft, more crumbly than Blue	Creamy white inside, marbled with blue-green veins of mold	Same as Blue blue veins of mold

Necessities of Life: Food ◄ 75

Spices and Herbs. With the popularity of international travel, the interest in foods containing spices and herbs has increased tremendously. As a result many spices and herbs from all over the world are now readily available for your recipes.

When adding spices and herbs to a recipe, start with a tested recipe to familiarize yourself with the flavors. Or, begin with $1/4$ teaspoon per 4 servings and then taste before adding more.

Since there is such a wide variety of herbs and spices, it's good to know something about each one before you go shopping. The guide to herbs and spices which follows will fill you in on the details.

SPICE & HERB CHART

Name	Seasoning Uses
Allspice	Fruits, cakes, cookies, beets, marinades, pot roasts, fruit and pumpkin pie, mincemeat.
Anise seed	Baked products: cakes, cookies, sweet breads; fruit cups and compotes.
Basil	Cheese spreads; tomato juice; minestrone, tomato and pea soup; baked or broiled fish; shrimp; salmon; cheese souffle, Spanish omelet; roast pork; liver; stews; meat pies; roast poultry; fricassee; goose; venison stuffings; eggplant; tomatoes; squash; onions; potato salad; tomato sauces.
Bay leaf	Tomato juice; pickling; tomato, beef, and chicken soup; court bouillon for poaching fish; pot roast; sauerbraten; smoked meats; chicken fricassee; roast duck; all venison; potatoes; carrots; beets; salad dressing; tomato sauces.
Caraway seeds	Baked products: rye bread, cake, rolls; cheese spreads; cole slaw; cabbage, sauerkraut, pork dishes, pot roasts.

Name	Seasoning Uses
Cardamon seed	Baked products: Danish coffee cakes, custard, cookies, pies; baked apples, fruit cup; melon; sweet potatoes; squash; pumpkin.
Celery seed	Soups, meat loaf, and stews, fish chowders, clam juice, tomato juice, potato salad, salad dressings, pickles, stuffings.
Chervil	Cream soups, omelets, salads.
Chives	Egg and cheese dishes, green vegetables, green salads, sour cream.
Cinnamon	Cakes, cookies, desserts, fruit pies, hot beverages, sweet potatoes, pumpkin, carrots, pickled fruits.
Cloves	Smoked meats especially ham, pickled or preserved fruits; apple, mince, pumpkin pie, hot beverages, pickles, cream of tomato or pea soup.
Coriander seed	Banana bread, cakes, cookies, lemon meringue pie.
Cumin seed	Stuffed eggs, cheese recipes, pork and sauerkraut.
Curry powder	Curry sauces for eggs, meat, fish, shrimp, salted nuts, creamed vegetables, mayonnaise.
Dill seed	Cucumber soup, stuffed eggs, veal and lamb recipes, fish sauces, cole slaw; vegetables: potatoes, sauerkraut, squash; dill pickles.
Ginger	Cookies, cakes, Indian puddings, fruits, poultry, pork, Chinese dishes, preserves, beets, and carrots.
Mace	Fish sauces, pound cake, cherry pie.
Marjoram	Paté; canape butter; spinach, clam and onion soup; broiled, baked or creamed

Name	Seasoning Uses
	fish; steamed clams; rarebits; omelets; scrambled eggs; cheese souffles, sausage, veal, lamb; meat loaf; chili; creamed chicken; stuffings, goose; venison; zucchini; spinach; eggplant; cabbage; mixed green salads; cream sauces; gravies.
Mint	Lamb; carrots, peas, green salads; chocolate recipes.
Mustard	Seed in pickles, salad dressing, marinades for meat and fish; powder in sauces, cream cheese dishes, vegetables, Chinese mustard, deviled eggs; ready mix for frankfurters, sauces as above.
Nutmeg	Cakes and cookies, stewed fruits, pumpkin pie; carrots, sweet potatoes, beans; eggnog, custards.
Oregano	Pizza; tomato juice; tomato, bean, onion, and vegetable soups; lobster; creamed fish, shellfish; boiled eggs; baked macaroni; cream and cottage cheese; roast pork, veal, lamb, meat loaf, chili, stuffings, rabbit, venison, goose, turkey; beans, mushrooms, onions, tomatoes, broccoli; avocado salad, seafood salad, green salads; tomato sauce, mushroom sauce, spaghetti sauce, barbecue sauce.
Paprika	Soups, eggs, fish, meat, and chicken recipes; salads and salad dressings, Hungarian goulash, chowders.
Parsley	Dips, soups, omelets, creamed dishes, sandwiches, salads, salad dressings.
Pepper, Black	Any non sweet dish that needs sparkle.
Pepper, Crushed red	Pizza, sausages, Italian dishes.

Name	Seasoning Uses
Pepper, White	Use as above where light color is preferable.
Poppy seed	Sprinkle on bread, rolls, coffee cake, pie crusts, noodles, salad dressings, cake fillings.
Rosemary	Fruit cup; turtle, chicken, pea, spinach soup; broiled and boiled fish; omelets; scrambled eggs; deviled eggs; ham loaf, stews, meat loaf, broiled meat, game birds, poultry, venison, rabbit; cauliflower, carrots, peas, beans; fruit salad; marinades; seafood sauces.
Saffron	Adds exotic color and flavor to rice, bread, fish, stews, Spanish dishes.
Sage	Cheese spreads; fish chowder; tomato soup; clams, fish stews; cottage, cream, or cheddar cheese; pork, roasts, sausage, stuffings, meat loafs, stuffings, rabbit, venison, goose, turkey; onions, corn, peas, beans; butter sauce for vegetables.
Sesame seed	Sprinkle on rolls, buns, cookies, candies, pie crust, salad dressing, fish, asparagus, beans, tomatoes.
Tarragon	Vegetable juices; seafood cocktail sauce; consomme, chicken and tomato soup; all fish and shellfish; omelets; scrambled eggs; roast beef, steaks, chops, sweetbreads, stuffings, stews, roast chicken and turkey; mushrooms, tomatoes, baked potato; flavor vinegar for salad dressing, mayonnaise, tartar sauce, hollandaise sauce, bearnaise sauce.
Thyme	Clam juice, sauerkraut juice, seafood cocktail sauce; Borscht, clam chowder, vegetable soup; all fish and shellfish; eggs; meat loaf, veal kidneys, boiled

Name	Seasoning Uses
	meat, game birds, chicken, venison, stuffings, stews; onions, baked beans, asparagus, beets, coleslaw; mayonnaise, mustard sauce, curry sauce, tomato sauce.
Turmeric	Egg, chicken, fish, and shellfish recipes; rice and macaroni dishes, potatoes.

Shelf Supplies. Stock your cupboard or pantry shelves with only those quantities of food that you plan to use within the next couple of months. Exceptions to this rule are the so-called staples which will keep longer. Spices and herbs lose considerable flavor during long storage periods. Vegetable oils once opened and stored in the refrigerator too long can become rancid. Those staples which have an indefinite shelf life can be purchased in large quantities to economize but only if you have adequate storage space.

Here is a suggested list of staples to keep on hand:

- Baking powder
- Baking soda
- Catsup
- Cereals
- Cocoa
- Coffee
- Cornstarch
- Extracts—vanilla, lemon, almond
- Flour—all purpose
- Gelatin—flavored, unflavored
- Herbs
- Molasses
- Paprika
- Pastas—spaghetti, macaroni
- Pepper—black, seasoned, cayenne
- Rice
- Salt—plain, seasoned, onion, garlic, celery
- Spices
- Sugar—granulated, confectioners' cube, brown
- Syrup—corn, maple
- Tea
- Vinegar

Here are canned and packaged items with a more limited shelf life:

Bouillon cubes
Canned goods
Baked beans
Corned beef hash
Fish, shellfish
Fruits
Juices — fruit, vegetable
Soups
Tomato paste, sauce
Vegetables
Crackers
Garlic cloves
Jams, jellies, spreads
Milk — evaporated,
    instant nonfat
    dry
Nuts
Oil — cooking, salad,
    olive
Onion — instant minced
    or flaked
Packaged mixes
Potatoes — packaged
    instant
Salad dressings
Sauces — chili, soy,
    Tabasco,
    Worcestershire

Kitchen Talk

As you learn your way around the kitchen, you may come across many unfamiliar terms related to foods and cooking. To make it a little easier for you, included here are three glossaries. The first, "Common Cooking Terms," defines words that tell you how to do certain cooking tasks such as whip, fry, or blend. The next includes foods and ingredients with which you may not be acquainted. And, for fledgling gourmets, the last lists some of the most commonly used foreign cooking terms and phrases with their definitions.

Common Cooking Terms

    bake — To cook in an oven.
    barbecue — To cook *over* direct heat, usually over an open fire.
    baste — A method of keeping food moist and adding

flavor during the cooking period by spooning a liquid or melted fat over it at various prescribed intervals.

beat — A vigorous stirring with an egg beater, spoon, or electric mixer.

blanch — To pour boiling water over a food and then drain quickly — or to parboil in water for a minute.

blend — To mix thoroughly.

boil — To cook in a liquid which has reached the bubbling point at 212° F (100° C).

bone — To remove the bones from meat or fish.

braise — A method of tenderizing tough cuts of meat by browning first in fat and then adding a small amount of liquid and cooking in a tightly covered container.

bread — To roll in crumbs, usually of bread or crackers.

broil — To cook under or over direct heat, under a broiler in the oven or over an open fire.

brown — To cook in fat until brown.

brush — To lightly coat the surface of food with a liquid or fat with a small brush.

caramelize — To melt sugar until it turns to a brown liquid.

chop — To cut into small pieces with a sharp, heavy knife.

cream — To beat to a smooth consistency.

cube — To cut into small squares.

cut in — To mix fat into flour when making pastry. Done with a pastry blender or a fork.

devil — To prepare a food by adding sharp seasonings and cooking with a crumb topping. Some deviled foods such as deviled eggs or deviled ham are prepared by dicing the main ingredient and then adding the sharp seasonings, but the cooking is eliminated.

dice — To cut into very small pieces.

disjoint — To cut fowl into pieces at the joints.

dot — To cover the surface with small bits of fat, usually butter or margarine.

dredge—To cover the surface of a food thoroughly with a dry substance such as flour or cornmeal.

dress—To mix a food with some type of seasoning, sauce, or "dressing" before serving.

dust—To cover a food very lightly with a dry ingredient like powdered sugar or flour.

fold—A method for combining two ingredients by turning one ingredient over into the other using a folding motion with a spoon or spatula. Beaten egg whites and whipped cream are usually "folded" with other ingredients.

fry—To cook in a pan on the top of the stove in a large amount of melted fat.

garnish—To decorate a food.

grate—To cut foods such as cheese or vegetables into tiny particles.

grill—See broil.

grind—To put through a grinder or blender which cuts the food into tiny particles.

julienne—To cut into long, thin strips.

knead—To mix with the hands. Bread mixtures are most often kneaded as one of the steps in preparation.

marinate—To soak a food in a liquid which usually contains herbs and other seasonings.

mince—To chop into very tiny pieces.

pan-broil—To cook in a skillet with very little, if any, fat.

parboil—To pre-cook for a short period of time in boiling salted water to reduce the total cooking time. Most often used with vegetables.

pare—To peel the skin off fruit or vegetables.

poach—To simmer gently in a hot liquid which just covers the food.

preheat—To heat the oven before using it, so an even temperature is maintained.

purée—To make a smooth paste by forcing food through a sieve or food mill.

reduce — To boil liquid until some of it evaporates to make a richer, more concentrated flavor.

render — To cook fat slowly until it melts.

roast — To cook in the oven in an open pan.

sauté — To cook in a pan on the stove-top with very little fat.

scald — To heat a liquid just to the boiling point without actually letting it boil.

score — To slash with a knife.

sear — To cook very quickly with high heat.

shred — To cut into thin slivers.

sift — To shake through a sieve to make particles finer.

simmer — To cook below boiling. The liquid used should barely bubble or move.

skim — To remove surface accumulations such as scum from a liquid.

sliver — To cut into long slices.

steam — To cook over boiling water in a tightly covered kettle with the food held above the water, usually on a rack.

stew — To cook slowly in liquid for a long time to blend and thoroughly mix all flavors.

stir — To mix ingredients by making a wide circular movement through them with a spoon.

truss — To tie a fowl with wings and legs held in place to maintain shape during cooking processes.

whip — To beat quickly until puffy.

Foods and Ingredients

barbecue sauce — A highly seasoned sauce used to baste food cooked over the direct heat of an open fire.

bouillon — The clear broth made by cooking meat, fish, poultry, or vegetables in liquid and then straining it. Also sold in cube and granular form in food stores.

bouquet garni—A small cheesecloth bag of selected herbs placed in a cooking liquid to add flavor while cooking. The bag and its contents is removed and discarded before serving.

broth—A thin soup; also, the liquid which remains after simmering and straining meats and vegetables. See bouillon, above.

capers—The tiny pickled buds of the caper shrub used primarily as a garnish with fish or lamb.

chutney—Sweet fruit pickle.

compote—A mixture of fruits, fresh or cooked.

condiment—An overall name for prepared sauces or seasonings, mustard, for example.

consommé—A clear meat broth, often highly seasoned.

cornstarch—A powdered starch used to thicken sauces, gravies.

croutons—Small cubes of bread which have been toasted. They can be made in your kitchen or purchased ready-made in a food store.

drippings—The juices that remain in the pan after roasting meat.

fillet or filet—A cut of fish or meat with the bones removed.

French mustard—Specially prepared, seasoned French mustards. Dijon is the most popular.

garlic—A member of the onion family which has a very strong flavor and odor. It can be purchased in salt or powder form as well as fresh.

gelatin—A powder used for thickening or forming a jelly-like substance from a liquid such as soup or broth. Also available in flavored versions which can be added to water to make great salads and desserts.

horseradish—A very strong-flavored plant root available whole or grated and used in hot, pungent sauces to accompany some fish, pork and beef dishes.

lard—The rendered (clarified) fat of pork sold com-

Necessities of Life: Food

mercially and used as shortening in pie crust dough and for cooking fat.

marinade — A seasoned sauce or dressing in which food, usually meat, is soaked prior to cooking and/or serving.

meringue — A pie and dessert topping made of stiffly beaten egg whites sweetened with sugar.

olive oil — Oil pressed from olives and used for cooking and in salad dressings. It is considered one of the best oils for these purposes.

pasta — An overall Italian name for foods made of flour and liquid, then dried and cut into various shapes like spaghetti, noodles, and shell macaroni.

paté — A paste made of meat, seafood, and sometimes vegetables. Used as a spread or garnish.

petits fours — Tiny fancy cakes or cookies.

pilaff — A rice dish. The rice is cooked with broth or wine and seasonings.

pimento — A sweet red pepper used as a garnish. Green olives often come stuffed with pimento.

rack — A rib section of meat.

ragout — French stew.

saddle — A cut of meat that includes the entire center section of an animal.

sauerkraut — Cabbage soaked in brine.

shish kebab — A method of cooking lamb (and sometimes other meats) on a skewer. Originated in the eastern Mediterranean.

shortening — Fat used in cooking.

soufflé — A puffy, baked mixture. Beaten egg whites are folded into other ingredients, then baked.

sour cream — A very thick commercial dairy product. Cream to which bacteria have been added. Used in baking and for dips and appetizers.

soy sauce — A sauce used primarily in Oriental cooking. It is made from soy beans and is sold bottled. Also used in marinades.

Spanish olives—Green olives stuffed with small pieces of pimento.

stock—The liquid in which a food has been cooked often used as the base for soups or gravies.

Tabasco—A very hot sauce to be used sparingly in hot, spicy foods.

tomato paste—A thickening agent for tomato sauces.

Worcestershire sauce—A pungent, brown sauce sold in bottles. Used to add flavoring to sauces, dressings, stews, and marinades.

Foreign Terms for Cooking and Dining

a la Grecque—Cooked in the Greek style, that is cooked in an oil and vinegar liquid with seasonings added.

a la mode—Topped with ice cream, as pie a la mode.

a la Russe—Cooked in the Russian style.

al dente—Describes foods cooked so they are still firm to bite. An Italian term.

aspic—A jellied glaze or broth.

au gratin—Baked with a bread-crumb topping.

au jus—Food served in its natural juices.

canapé—A toasted or fried slice of bread spread with a highly seasoned food and used as an appetizer. See hors d'oeuvre, below.

cassoulet—A casserole of French origin. Usually contains a mixture of white beans and goose or duckling.

champignons—Mushrooms.

crême—Cream.

crepe—A thin French pancake, usually rolled and filled with fruit or a meat mixture and sauce.

demitasse—A small cup of black coffee.

diable—Deviled.

duchesse—Potatoes which have been cooked, mixed with egg, and then forced through a pastry tube.

éclair—A pastry filled with custard or whipped cream and topped with frosting.

en brochette—Cooked on a skewer.

en coquilles—Cooked in the shell.

entrée—The main dish of the meal.

fines herbes—Herbs chopped and mixed together and used for seasoning. The most common mixture includes parsley, chives, and tarragon.

flambé—To pour liquor over a food before lighting a fire to it. The American term for this process is blaze.

fondue—A melted food or mixture. Cheese fondue is probably the most common form in the United States.

fricassée—Braised meats or poultry. See braise under "Common Cooking terms."

glacé—Frozen dessert; ice cream.

hors d'oeuvre—Small finger foods usually served with cocktails or other beverages, often before a meal. Called appetizers in English.

jardinère—Mixed vegetables served in their own cooking juice.

légumes—Vegetables.

lyonnaise—Cooked with onions.

pâté de foie gras—A paste made of goose livers.

patisserie—Pastry.

petits pois—Tiny green peas.

pois—Peas.

potage—Soup.

poulet—Chicken.

ragout—Thick stew, highly seasoned.

ratatouille—A stew made of mixed vegetables. It usually contains eggplant and tomatoes cooked in olive oil.

truffles—A fungi similar to mushrooms and used in similar ways.

vichyssoise—A cream soup made of potatoes and usually served ice cold.

vinaigrette — A marinade made of oil and vinegar and herbs. Used primarily on vegetables.

Safety in the Kitchen

Because electricity, gas, and water are used extensively in any kitchen, a few safety rules are in order. It is most important that appliances be used in accordance with the instructions that accompany them. If the tenant prior to you didn't leave instruction manuals behind for the dishwasher, stove, and refrigerator, write to the manufacturers for copies. State the model and serial number (usually on the back). Be sure to keep instruction booklets and guarantees and/or warranties for all small electric appliances, too.

Food can be potentially dangerous, too. Warm, moist food is an excellent medium for the growth of bacteria which can cause upset stomach, cramps, diarrhea, and even death. But you can do something to prevent them.

Oven Safety

1. To light a gas oven, open the oven door first, then light the match and place near pilot light opening, then turn on the gas.
2. Turn off the oven, burners, and broiler when cooking is completed. Check all controls before going to bed or leaving the apartment.
3. Keep stove burners clean. Wipe up spills immediately. Caked-on foods are a potential fire hazard.
4. Use thick hot pads to handle anything that has been in the oven or on the top of the stove.
5. Check the pilot lights on gas stoves periodically to be sure they're lit, especially if you smell gas. If pilots are lit, and gas odor persists, there may be

a gas leak. Call the building superintendent *immediately* for repairs.
6. Boil water and cook in hot fat in pans of ample size so liquids and/or grease do not splash over the sides.
7. If you must leave the kitchen in the midst of cooking something on the top of the stove, turn off the burner.
8. Put out kitchen fires by smothering flames with flour or baking soda. Water only makes most kitchen fires worse.
9. Open windows for ventilation while cleaning oven with aerosol spray cleaners. Follow package instructions *explicitly!*
10. Don't store matches, aerosol spray cans, or any other flammable materials near or above the oven where they could fall into an open flame.
11. Don't hang dish towels near the stove.
12. Don't touch water and an electric stove, light switch, or other live electric appliance at the same time. A bad shock—even a fatal one—awaits.
13. Don't use an automatic timing device in an electric oven that turns it on while you're away. For safety's sake, it's not a good idea to use the oven when no one is home.

Safety Tips for Other Appliances

1. Unplug all electric appliances when not in use.
2. Check the cords and plugs of all electric appliances periodically for exposed wiring or frayed cords. Replace worn parts immediately.
3. If you must open the dishwasher once the cycle has started, open the door just a crack and allow steam to escape before reaching inside.
4. Don't turn on the dishwasher when you plan to be away during the cycle. Mechanical or electrical

failure might mean coming home to a kitchen full of suds — or worse!
5. Don't stick objects, especially those made of metal, into a toaster, unless it is unplugged.

Safety with Sharp Objects

1. Store sharp knives and other sharp utensils in one place, preferably in a secure place away from the reach of children. Avoid hanging them on the wall since they can fall easily.
2. Be sure to close all cupboard doors, immediately.
3. Wash knives and sharp kitchen tools *one at a time*. Do not drop them into the dishwasher.
4. If you break glassware in the dishwater, drain water, then remove glass.
5. Vacuum up broken glass immediately. If vacuum is unavailable, sweep thoroughly and go over the area with a dampened paper towel.
6. To avoid shattering glassware, do not subject it to extremes in temperature. For example, do not place a glass baking dish in cold water just after removing it from the oven.

Food Safety

1. Wash your hands before and after handling raw foods. Wash all cutting surfaces and utensils with soap and water after use.
2. Put all perishable and frozen foods in refrigerator as soon as possible after shopping. Wrap meats and poultry in freezer paper or plastic wrap and aluminum foil. Uncooked meat which has been properly refrigerated for three days or less can be frozen. Use immediately, otherwise.

3. Defrost foods in the refrigerator, *not* at room temperature. Place on a plate or in a pan to prevent dripping into other foods.
4. Do not thaw and refreeze frozen meats, fish, poultry and vegetables without cooking them first.
5. Store leftover foods in refrigerator, promptly. Cool in small quantities and shallow layers so the temperature of the food is brought down to refrigerator temperature in 2 to 3 hours.
6. Do not use any foodstuff that looks or smells bad.
7. Don't use canned foods in bulging cans or with bulging lids on glass jars. If it's commercially canned food, return it to the supermarket where you bought it and inform your local health official. It could save lives.
8. Put prepared foods in refrigerator until ready to serve. All foodstuffs with an egg or dairy base must be refrigerated.
9. If you have a pet, keep its feeding dishes, toys, and bedding out of the kitchen.
10. Use a meat thermometer to make sure interior is cooked thoroughly (at least 175 to 185° F for poultry, 170° F for fresh pork).
11. Remove dressing (stuffing) from meat, fish, and poultry before refrigerating. Refrigerate immediately and use leftovers within a day or two.
12. Don't store foods, especially acidic foods (orange juice, for example), in pottery unless you know for sure it has a glaze which contains no lead.

Kitchen Abbreviations and Measures

Just in case you've never been in a kitchen, the following charts will be invaluable to you.

COMMON KITCHEN ABBREVIATIONS

	Abbreviation
teaspoon	tsp
tablespoon	T or tbs
cup	c
ounce	oz
pint	pt
quart	qt
liter	l
milliliter	ml
gram	g
kilogram	kg
meter	m
centimeter	cm

STANDARD WEIGHTS AND MEASURES

	Volume in Customary Units	Approximate Metric Equivalents
A dash	8 drops	8 drops
1 teaspoon	60 drops	5 milliliters
1 tablespoon	3 teaspoons	15 milliliters
1 fluid ounce	2 tablespoons	30 milliliters
¼ cup	4 tablespoons	60 milliliters
⅓ cup	5⅓ tablespoons	80 milliliters
1 cup	16 tablespoons or 8 fluid ounces	240 milliliters
1 pint	2 cups	475 milliliters
1 quart	2 pints	.95 liters
1 gallon	4 quarts	3.8 liters
	Weight in Customary Units	Approximate Metric Equivalents
1 pound	16 ounces	460 grams

Outdoor Cooking

Barbecuing is one of the most entertaining forms of cooking. There must be a fire bed through which air can circulate and a grill on which to lay the food. You can use starter fluids available in markets. Or lay the fire with crumpled paper; add dry twigs and set the paper aflame. When the twigs catch fire, cover them with a single layer of charcoal or charcoal briquettes. After five minutes add a second layer of charcoal. Then in another five minutes add a third layer.

The fire should cover an area just large enough to accommodate the food to be cooked. Do not begin to cook until the coals have an ashy gray coat.

Barbecuing Equipment

Broiling basket or hinged broiler—for small fish or smaller cuts of meat.
Asbestos gloves
Tongs for turning meat (to avoid piercing it)
Long handled fork and spatula turner
Clothes sprinkler (handy for controlling flames caused by dripping fat)
Brush for basting
Carving fork, knife and board
Skillet
Small pan for basting sauce
Skewers

NECESSITIES OF LIFE: CLOTHING

Wardrobe Psychology

Buying clothes is one of the purest ego adventures that you can experience. So whenever the occasion arises, enjoy it to its fullest, within budgetary limitations of course. Whether you realize it or not, clothes are an outlet for a mixture of emotions. According to the Stanford Research Institute, there are several key values which will have a major impact upon the Clothing and Accessories Industry in the years to come: individuality, experimentation, self-centeredness, direct experience, appreciation of diversity, taste, sense of security, naturalism, pleasure, materialism, success, and conformity.

Whether one or several of these factors motivates you when you buy something for yourself, the fact is that apparel and accessory designs are freer than ever. It's marvelous! Perhaps the most significant turning point, the championship moment for self-expression in clothing and self destiny, occurred in 1970. American women were *told* by fashion designers and the press that they would have to accept the midi skirt, no questions asked. The unanticipated happened. Women by the thousands refused to knuckle under. Now we have an unhampered coexistence of varying skirt lengths, different looks. We are at the summit. Not only women, but men as well. Just five years ago who would have ever thought that denim would become a fashion fabric?

It seems as though we are always in need of clothes. Sometimes the need is more imagined than real. Let's face it. Every one of us, at one time or another, has rationalized a new suit or dress. It's a permissable game as long as it doesn't become too self-indulgent. And occasionally it works like a prescription. Clothes can uplift the spirit. But like any tonic, they can become ineffective and highly expensive if relied upon too often.

When the need is definitely real, you should still treat it as a want. In other words, satisfy yourself while you're filling a gap in your wardrobe. Don't force your buying decisions. Rash purchases are often wasteful. If you're not sure, pass it up. Never shop on-the-run if you can possibly avoid it. Pin down what you'll be shopping for *before* you go shopping. Then allot your time accordingly. However, if you are shopping for pants, and a sweater you really need is on sale, try to take advantage of it. Relaxation adds to the shopping experience, and it puts you in the right frame of mind to make the right decisions.

Developing a Wardrobe

Every wardrobe should have balance. Most of us have weaknesses for certain types of clothing or accessories. If you do, then some self-discipline is in order. Don't overstock one segment of your wardrobe at the expense of other segments.

Plan your wardrobe according to your lifestyle. Give importance to business clothes but don't ignore the dress-up or casual parts of your life.

We work to make our leisure time as comfortable as possible. It would be a shame not to have a wardrobe to add to this sense of comfort.

Very often, too, business tension can be relieved if you have something nice and different to slip into when you get home. A simple pair of jeans or a pair of corduroy pants very often can communicate a feeling of relaxation. Whatever your preference, you should have it (them) waiting for you in your closet for those times when you want to mentally and physically change roles.

Seasonal and travel clothes need consideration, too. But try to spend within a framework of usage and relative importance. It's great to look your best on vacation or at a resort. But it can be depressing or disappointing, if you return home to a regular wardrobe that's fair-to-poor. Thus, your wardrobe should manifest appropriate respect for each part of your lifestyle. When it does, your life will have an important degree of consistency.

In developing your wardrobe here are some things to think about:

1. Don't skimp on important things like a coat or shoes or anything you wear a lot. In the long run, you'll save on quality.
2. Know your taste in clothes (many people don't). Take time to think about the kinds of clothing left hanging in the closet and the kind that you're always wearing. *Closet hangers* are bad purchases. When you recognize what they are, you won't make the same mistake twice, and you'll save yourself a lot of money.

3. Buy one or two pairs of good, well-made, well-fitting pants or slacks in basic colors and styles. Then buy jackets and shirts or blouses, both dressy and casual, to go with them. Even though you keep wearing the same pants, you'll look different because of the varying combinations.
4. Don't buy something that needs to be altered too much, especially things on sale that aren't really your size. Too much altering changes the proportion of clothes and they'll never look right.
5. Check sales for out-of-season bargains. Most stores have good sales at the end of the season to make room for next season's merchandise. But don't buy anything you don't really need. It just might become another *closet hanger.*
6. If you've bought several very satisfactory things from one store, manufacturer, or designer, look for more from the same source.
7. Be aware of the upkeep of anything you buy before you purchase. Suede, for example, is expensive to have cleaned.
8. Whenever possible buy fabrics that can be worn through all the seasons. This will reduce, perhaps eliminate the need for buying a new wardrobe several times a year. Synthetic blends, corduroys, and light knits are some of the excellent all-year-round fabrics.
9. Spend the time and/or money to keep clothes and shoes in good repair. And don't wait too long to have repairs done. The damage may become irreparable.
10. Shop in stores that have a good return or exchange policy.
11. If there are clothing manufacturers in your area, they may have outlets where they sell their merchandise, most often at discount. They're worth checking!

CLOTHES TO FIT THE FIGURE

Here are a few pointers on how to create visual illusions with clothing to complement your body structure.

Build	Men	Women
Short	Pin stripes and vertical lines in sport shirts and slacks.	Choose clothes with vertical lines. Heels add height but don't overdo it. Hairstyles can also increase apparent height.
Tall	Sports coats and contrasting pants will help break up appearance of extreme height. Tight-fitting pants and jackets will make you seem even taller.	Wear outfits that break in the middle and have top and bottom contrasting colors. Slim heels. Hats and hairdos should not add inches.
Overweight	Be well-tailored. Don't let clothes show overweight areas noticeably. Double-breasted jackets tend to give a thinning appearance. Black and navy are slimming colors.	Avoid large prints and fabrics like jersey which cling and reveal bulges. Long earrings are a good idea—they tend to lengthen the neck. Black and navy are good colors.
Thin	You have fewer problems. Can wear all fabrics, even the heavy ones, without fear of looking too bulky. If arms are too thin, wear long sleeves as much as possible.	You can wear almost all clothes. If certain features are too prominent, deemphasize them. For example, long neck bones can be hidden with a scarf, turtleneck or high collar. Avoid a low neckline. Nubby materials will give added weight.
Average	Emphasize your good features. Minimize poorer features. You have a wide range of styles to choose from.	Same. Do not wear a mini skirt if you have heavy legs. Fit the fashion to your body type.

Extra Tips

1. Neatness counts—all clothes should fit well. If you're putting on or taking off weight have alterations made.
2. When a woman is chic or a man is a good dresser, they are usually up-to-date on fashion but know how to let their individuality show in their appearance.
3. Jewelry, like everything else, should not be overdone. Gross use of jewelry doesn't impress, it signifies poor taste. Rings look best on long, slender fingers. Clanking jewelry can be disruptive and irritating, especially on the job.
4. *Suitability* is the key to dressing. Each body has its assets and liabilities. Don't indiscriminately embrace a new fashion if it does not suit your body (case in point: women with heavy legs should avoid mini skirts; people with double chins should avoid turtle necks).
5. Go lightly with cologne or perfume. A soft fragrance is usually more pleasing than an overpowering one.

Labels

Today, with the great number of textiles and materials being used in the fabrication of garments, it's often impossible for a consumer to know exactly what fiber or combination of fibers he or she is buying.

To protect your interest, and your purchasing dollar, the FTC requires that every garment have a label that will provide this information. According to the FTC regulations listed in its Buyer's Guide No. 6 (Title: *Look For That Label*), this label should be positioned so that you can find it easily. And, either on or close to the label should be the name or code number of the manufacturer who is responsible for the validity of the label.

Here are the labels that you should demand and read. They are categorized by content.

Blends. Labels must set forth the percentages and generic names (family names) of all fibers present in the products if these fibers amount to 5% or more of the total. This applies to wool, reused wool, and all fibers other than wool.

This prevents false advertising or labeling that would lead us to believe that a garment is made of an expensive material, when the expensive material is only a small percentage of the blend.

Wool. Reprocessed wool refers to fibers made from wool that has never been woven or felted into a wool product used by a consumer. Reused wool means fiber reclaimed from woolen products which consumers have used.

Wool is the fiber from the fleece of the sheep or lamb or the hair of the Angora or Kashmir (Cashmere) goat (and may include the so-called specialty fibers from the hair of the alpaca, camel, llama or vicuna) which has never been reclaimed from any woven or felted wool product. Virgin or new wool means wool fiber which has never been used or made into anything before.

Man-Made Textiles. There are now over 700 trade names for manufactured fibers which results in a lot of consumer confusion. To help simplify matters, the FTC has grouped them into 17 generic groups. This makes it easier to know what kind of fabric you are buying, its advantages, and its disadvantages.

The categories are: acetate, acrylic, anidex, azlon,

glass, metallic, modacrylic, nylon, nytril, olefin, polyester, rayon, rubber, saran, spandex, vinal, and vinyon.

A generic name cannot be used if the fiber is less than 5% of the total fabric. The only exception to this rule is when the fiber has functional significance. Then there could be a statement on the label such as "4% spandex for elasticity."

Furs. Fur labels must list several things including: 1) the true English name of the animal producing the fur; 2) the country of origin if the fur is imported; 3) whether the fur product is dyed, bleached, artificially colored, or its natural color; 4) whether it is composed of paws, bellies, scrap pieces, or waste furs. The label must also show the name or registered identification number of the manufacturer or distributor.

Care Labels. Care labels indicate how to wash, bleach, dry, iron, or dry clean. When you're buying, be sure to look for them. If they can't be seen through the packaging, then the packaging must have the necessary instructions printed on it according to FTC regulations (Buyers' Guide No. 10).

Some products *not* covered by the FTC Care Labeling regulations are hosiery,* headwear, handwear, footwear, disposable items, washable garments intended to retail for $3 or less, fur and leather items, purely decorative or ornamental items, remnants cut and shipped by the manufacturer and see-through or other items whose appearance would be substantially impaired by a label such as a chiffon scarf.

To supplement labeling information, see the "Fiber Care Chart" which outlines care techniques for the basic fibers that you will encounter.

* Care labels must accompany some sheer hosiery products and those that color bleed.

Taking Care of Your Wardrobe

In day-to-day living, accidents happen and stains result. Often they require the services of a professional cleaner. But, with a little self-sufficiency, some acquired skill, and a touch of elbow grease, you can handle many of them yourself.

For best results, you should always deal with stains at once. If a stain is of unknown origin but seems nongreasy, soak it in cold water, then wash in warm suds. If it seems greasy, sponge with carbon tetrachloride or a similar dry-cleaning solvent, then wash.

Always try any chemicals used in stain removal on the inside of a hem or other inconspicuous place. If the results are not satisfactory, don't go any further. See our "Stain Removal Chart" (page 107) for specific instructions.

FIBER CARE CHART°

Fiber	General Care	Special Instructions
acetate	Usually dry clean. If labeled for washing, wash by hand in warm water and mild suds. Don't wring or twist, don't soak colored fabrics. Press while slightly damp on wrong side with cool iron or use a press cloth on the right side.	Keep away from acetone, nail polish remover, for example. It dissolves acetate.
acrylic	Most items should be washed in warm water by hand. Squeeze out water, don't wring. Smooth item and dry on hanger. If labeled for machine washing, use	Dry knitted items flat (they'll stretch otherwise). Static electricity build-up can be reduced by using fabric softener in every four or five washings, whether

° Reprinted from The Butterick Fabric Handbook.

FIBER CARE CHART (continued)

Fiber	General Care	Special Instructions
	warm water, machine dry at low, and remove from dryer as soon as tumbling cycle is over.	by hand or machine. (Not more often—it tends to dull clothes.)
anidex	May be washed or dry cleaned depending on fibers used with it. May be tumbled or drip dried. Use a moderate heat setting if ironing is necessary.	This elastic man-made fiber (unlike spandex) is not damaged by chlorine bleach.
cotton	Most 100% cottons can be washed by machine at the regular cycle with hot water, and dried at the regular setting. Use chlorine bleach only on whites and colored fabrics which you have tested for color retention. High temperature iron setting may be used. Wash cotton knits by hand to avoid excessive shrinkage.	Don't assume that all cotton fabrics are color-fast. Check the label or test a small portion; if the color runs, have the item dry cleaned.
glass fibers	Wash only by hand and hang to dry while wet.	Be careful in washing, slivers of glass can injure hands.
linen	Machine wash in hot water, dry at regular cycle. Dark colors should be washed in water of a lower temperature to keep them from fading. Dry cleaning is especially satisfactory for color and shape retention of linens.	Do not bleach colored linens.

FIBER CARE CHART (continued)

Fiber	General Care	Special Instructions
modacrylic	Pile garments (fake furs, for instance) should be dry cleaned or cleaned commercially by the fur method. Some items are washable. Machine wash in warm water, use low setting of dryer and remove items promptly.	A fabric softener will reduce static electricity in the washable items. Use lowest possible setting when ironing is necessary; modacrylic is extremely sensitive to heat.
nylon	Most items can be machine washed in warm water and tumble dried at low setting. Remove from dryer promptly to avoid heat-set wrinkles. If ironing is desired, use only a warm iron. Nylon tends to pick up colors from other fabrics if not washed separately. Sponge upholstery and rugs or use special cleaners for these items.	Static electricity can be reduced by the use of fabric softener in every four or five washings.
olefin	Machine wash in lukewarm water, machine dry only at lowest setting. Remove from dryer as soon as tumbling stops. Do not dry in a commercial or laundromat type gas-fired dryer. In blends, use lowest possible setting when ironing. Never iron 100% olefin. Stains on rugs, carpets, and upholstery can be sponged clean.	Notice cautions on temperature for drying and ironing.

Necessities of Life: Clothing ◄ 105

FIBER CARE CHART (continued)

Fiber	General Care	Special Instructions
polyester	Machine washing at a warm setting with drying at a low temperature is recommended for polyester. Remove items from the dryer promptly to avoid heat-set wrinkles. Iron with a moderately warm iron. Some white polyesters pick up color from other fabrics; wash separately if this would be objectionable. Polyester fabrics can be dry cleaned but watch prints — some color substances often used on printed polyesters are injured by dry cleaning.	Avoid over-drying of polyester and especially of polyester knits — it will give the effect of shrinkage. Notice caution on dry cleaning of polyesters.
rayon	Dry cleaning is definitely safest for rayon; however, if washing, wash by hand in lukewarm water. Do not wring or twist, and don't use chlorine bleach as some finishes on rayon are chlorine retentive which leads to yellowing and loss of strength. Smooth the item, hang on hanger to dry, press while still damp on the wrong side with a moderate iron or use a pressing cloth on the right side.	Notice caution on the use of chlorine bleach.
saran	Saran fibers are usually found domestically only	

FIBER CARE CHART (continued)

Fiber	General Care	Special Instructions
	on garden furniture; sponge or hose clean.	
silk	Dry cleaning is best for silk, although some silks can be hand washed (only if so labeled). Squeeze suds through fabric, do not wring or twist. Iron on the wrong side. To avoid water spotting (marks made by drops of water) do not use steam when pressing silk. Iron at medium temperature.	Never use chlorine bleach on silk.
spandex	Wash by hand or machine in lukewarm water, drip dry or dry at low temperature by machine.	Do not use chlorine bleach as spandex is chlorine retentive causing yellowing and loss of strength. Avoid ironing. If ironing is essential, iron rapidly at the lowest possible temperature setting. Spandex slowly disintegrates from heat.
triacetate	Machine wash and dry at normal hot settings, except pleated items, which should be hand washed. A high iron temperature may be used.	Keep away from acetone — see caution for acetate.
vinyon	Sponge vinyon clean.	
wool	Woven woolens should be dry cleaned, except for those labeled "washable." Follow care in-	Never use chlorine bleach on wool. Dry knits flat to avoid stretching.

FIBER CARE CHART (continued)

Fiber	General Care	Special Instructions
	structions on such woolens exactly. Machine-made knitted woolens should also be dry cleaned, unless labeled "washable," in which case follow label instructions. The dry cleaner should be told these fabrics are woolens to ensure the proper technique is used in cleaning and drying. Hand wash socks, mittens, and hand-knit items in lukewarm or cold water using special soap for wool.	

STAIN REMOVAL[*]

Stain	Removal Method
ballpoint pen ink	Ballpoint pen ink comes out quite easily when sponged with rubbing alcohol. On a washable fabric, any stain which remains should be rubbed with soap or a detergent and then the fabric should be washed. The same method should be used on non-washable items, followed by sponging with a mild detergent solution of 1 teaspoon detergent to 1 cup of water.
blood	Washable fabrics should be soaked in cold water immediately. If they do not respond to cold water, an enzyme presoak (when available) should be used. The fabrics should then be washed in

[*] Reprinted from The Butterick Fabric Handbook.

STAIN REMOVAL (continued)

Stain	Removal Method
	the usual way. Non-washable items should be sponged with cold water followed by a mild detergent solution (1 teaspoon detergent to 1 cup of water). If the detergent solution doesn't work, try a solution of 1 tablespoon ammonia in a cup of water—and if that changes the color of the item, follow it up by sponging with ¼ cup white vinegar in 1 cup of water to bring back the original color. Test both the ammonia solution and the vinegar solution in some inconspicuous spot before using on the stain.
candle wax	Follow instructions for chewing gum, below.
chewing gum	Chewing gum can be removed from most fabrics if it is first hardened by rubbing it with an ice cube and then scraped off with a blunt knife or your fingernail. This takes time and patience but it does work. In desperate cases, you can try sponging the gum with a nonflammable cleaning fluid, but this can spread the stain.
coffee, tea	Simple washing will usually remove coffee and tea stains on washable fabrics. On non-washable fabrics, sponge with cold water first, then try mild detergent solution of 1 teaspoon detergent to 1 cup of water.
cream, milk	Washing will remove cream and milk from washable fabrics. On non-washable fabrics, start by wiping with a damp sponge. If that fails, shake cornstarch or white talcum powder onto the stain, allow to dry thoroughly, then use a brush or vacuum to remove the residue.

STAIN REMOVAL (continued)

Stain	Removal Method
greasy stains, including lipstick, tar	Start by following the ice-cube method given for chewing gum, then use lighter fluid to remove remaining stain on both washable and non-washable fabrics.
nail polish	Nail polish remover will remove nail polish from most fabrics, but NEVER use it on acetate or triacetate. On these fabrics, try to scrape the polish off with a blunt knife or fingernail.
paint (oil based)	See instructions for nail polish, above.
paint (water based)	If the paint is still wet, sponge with water trying not to spread the stain further. If the paint is dry, nothing (including dry cleaning) will get it out, but you may be able to scrape some off the surface with a blunt knife or your fingernail.
perspiration	Certain man-made fibers seem to hold perspiration odors longer than other fabrics; although a stain will come out with washing, the odor may not. Rub the area of the odor with a deodorant soap before washing.
urine, vomit, mucous	On washable fabrics, soak in an enzyme pre-soak (if possible) then wash using a suitable bleach (chlorine or oxygen type). On non-washable items, such as rugs, sponge first with mild detergent solution (1 teaspoon detergent to a cup of water) and rinse. If that doesn't work, try white vinegar solution—$1/4$ cup white vinegar to 1 cup water. If this solution changes the color, try to neutralize it with an ammonia solution of 1 tablespoon ammonia to 1 cup water. Test both the ammonia solution and the vinegar solution in an inconspicuous spot before using on the stain.

Laundering Tips. When using a washing machine, here are some tips to help you get the best results:

1. Add clothes a minute or two *after* the detergent has been mixed with wash water. This will give the detergent sufficient time to soften the water. And, when most of the "hard" minerals are precipitated out of the water, colors will appear brighter.
2. Use the hottest water suitable for the fabric. This should be at least 140° F (60° C) for colorfast cottons. Certain fabrics should not be washed in hot water. So, once again, check care labels.
3. If you are unsure about colorfastness, dissolve a teaspoon of detergent in a cup of hot water. Put a few drops of this hot solution on a seam or another hidden area of the garment and let sit for 5 minutes. Rinse and check for any color change.
4. To prevent permanent press fabrics from wrinkling, set the washing machine for special wash 'n wear or permanent press — or warm water and cold rinse. Dry in automatic dryer if possible and remove garments as soon as they're dry so wrinkles do not "set."
5. Always separate white fabrics from colored fabrics.

Care of Leather. There are two types of leather that you should be aware of because they require different cleaning techniques. The first is smooth leather, either shiny or matte finish and the second is suede or those leathers that have a suede look, such as chamois, buckskin, and shearling.

To remove surface dirt from smooth leather, wipe with a damp cloth dipped in mild soap and water, pat dry, dust lightly with baby powder, then rub with a clean cloth.

For suede, or suede-like leather, use a sponge or brush (plastic or nylon), to rub against the grain to raise the nap. For major stains like grease, ink, or sugar take it to a dry cleaner who specializes in leather. Also, before storing a suede garment have it professionally cleaned, then hang it on a contoured or padded hanger to keep the suede shoulder line in shape, and drape a cloth across the shoulders so that surface dust won't darken the color. Empty all leather and suede pockets to prevent sags or bulges. And *don't* use airtight garment bags. They can discolor leather and suede.

For pressing, use a rayon or low setting on your iron, *no steam,* and never place the iron directly on leather. Use a press cloth of heavy wrapping paper and work iron lightly up and down.

Care of Boots. Leather is an animal skin and, like your own, it needs cleaning and moisturizing. For delicate leathers like kidskin, a neutral cream is a good cleaning-moisturizing agent. Saddle soap works best on heavy leathers but can dull the finish and even crack the surface on delicate leathers.

Suede boots or shoes need brushing with very fine sandpaper or a dry sponge.

For vinyl and cloth boots or shoes, wipe with a sponge dampened in non-detergent soap. To repel stains spray with a silicone spray.

To prevent tarnish or chips on metal buttons and/or buckles, paint them with clear nail polish.

Always clean boots or shoes before summer storage. And when you store them. Stuff them with newspaper or dress cardboard to keep them in shape for the next season. Cover boots for the summer months.

Basic Clothing Repairs. Just a few quick lessons that may save your day, or at least help you cope with an emergency that suddenly may befall you before a date or an important engagement.

Sewing on Buttons, Snaps, and Hooks and Eyes. Since thread for sewing buttons must withstand wear, use buttonhole twist, button and carpet thread, heavy-duty thread, or a double strand of cotton thread coated with beeswax. Use an 18" length to avoid tangles. Securely fasten thread on outside of garment at marking.

The names of buttons correspond to the way they are attached to garment, sew-through and shank.

Sew-Through Buttons (buttons with two or four holes), unless used for trims, should have a thread shank to prevent the fabric around the closure from being distorted. It should be as long as the garment is thick at buttonhole, plus a scant $1/8$" for movement. Form shank by putting a toothpick or bobby pin over button between holes; sew over object when attaching button.

When button is secure, remove object, and wind thread tightly under button to form shank; securely fasten thread to shank.

Shank Buttons are attached with small stitches sewn through the built-in shank (loop). Align shank with buttonhole so threads will be parallel to opening edge. An additional thread shank may be needed for very thick fabric.

Reinforced Buttons are used for coats, suits, or delicate fabrics. For coats, place a small flat button on inside of garment directly under outer button and sew from one to the other, making thread shanks as needed. On delicate fabrics, substitute a small folded square of ribbon seam binding; at openings, place it between garment and facing.

Snaps and Hooks and Eyes are quick, easy closures. When positioning a snap, remember that the ball section of the snap, the part with protruding knob, should be sewn to the overlapping garment section; the socket section, the one with the indentation, is applied to the underlapping section. Sew the snap sections in place with small, close stitches taking four or five stitches in each hole. Secure thread tightly.

Hooks will withstand the strain of body movement and give a smooth finish. Sew the hook to the overlapping section of the garment and attach the eye or loop directly be-

BASIC WARDROBE REPAIRS

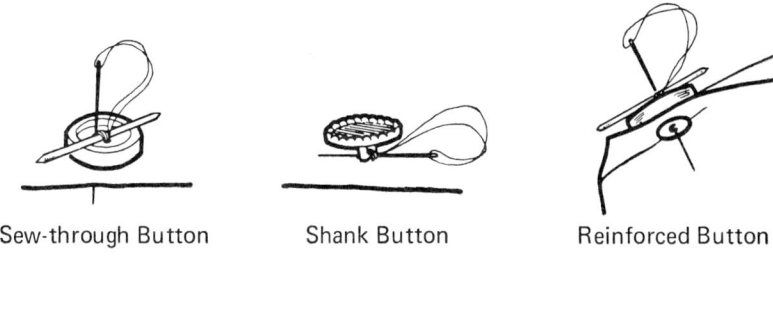

Sew-through Button Shank Button Reinforced Button

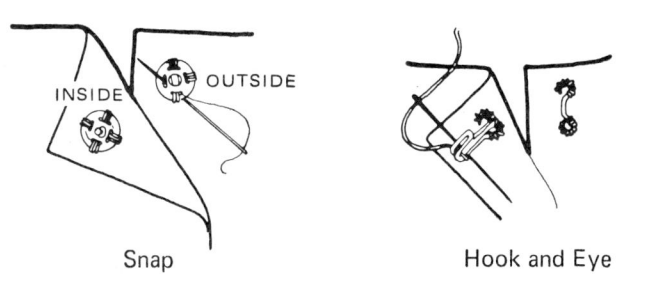

Snap Hook and Eye

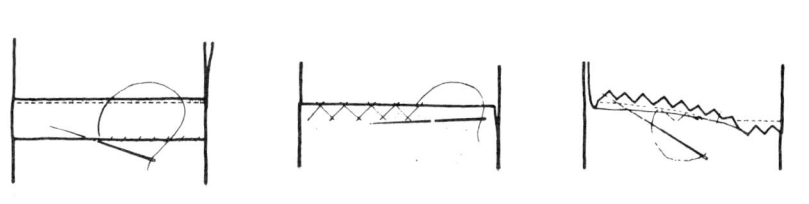

Hemming Stitch Catchstitch Blind Stitch

neath the hook on the underlapping garment section. Secure with tiny stitches as described for snaps, above.

Hemming

Hemming stitch is for hems finished with seam binding. Take a tiny stitch in the garment, then bring needle diagonally through seam binding or hem edge. Take all stitches in this manner, spacing them about ¼" apart.

Catchstitch holds two layers of fabric in place flexibly. Use it to hem stretchy fabrics. Work from left to right, taking a small horizontal stitch from right to left in the upper layer of fabric. Just beyond the edge of the upper layer, take an identical stitch diagonally from the first in the under layer. Sew in a loose zigzag manner.

Blindstitch makes an inconspicuous hem. It makes a blind hem — one in which stitches can't be seen from either side of garment. Take a small horizontal stitch through one thread of garment. Then pick up a thread of hem diagonally above previous stitch. Work in a zigzag manner. Don't pull stitches too tight; every 4 or 5 inches, stretch the blindstitched area and take a few extra stitches in the hem allowance (not the garment) for a more durable, rip-proof hem.

These are just quick pointers. Sewing and maintaining your clothes is a subject that is worthy of a book(s) all by itself. So for the self-sufficient single, male or female, we recommend Butterick's *Ready Set Sew*. It has all the basics written and illustrated so that even the beginner can learn from it quickly.

For the more sophisticated single sewer, we recommend *The Vogue Sewing Book* and *The Vogue Sewing Book of Fitting, Alterations, and Adjustments*. Another handy reference for your bookshelf is *The Butterick Fabric Handbook, A Consumer's Guide To Fabrics For Clothing and Home Furnishings*.

FINANCIAL AND LEGAL NITTY GRITTY

Managing Your Money

Of great concern to everyone these days is the shrinking purchasing power of the dollar. How can you stretch it and thereby get the most value out of it? According to First National City Bank (Consumer Views, Vol. V, No. 8) this is really a multiple question. Not only must you pay higher prices, you must also save something for tomorrow and for unforseen emergencies. At the same time you must have something left over so you can get some fun out of life or else what's the sense in working. First National City asked a number of bankers, the people who make a living out of managing money, how they are coping with the pressures of inflation. Their answers are interesting and valuable.

Setting Priorities. Before buying anything, make a distinction between what's nice and what's necessary. This is strictly a personal evaluation. Whereas a car might be nice for someone who will use it to get away on weekends, it might be absolutely essential to another person who will use it to make business calls.

Furthermore, there are different price levels to consider. Some products are fancier or more complex than others. If you are shopping for a television set, you must decide on color versus black & white, on a 16" screen versus a 19" screen. In the end, your ultimate decision should be based on the value of the product in terms of the importance it will play in your life. If you make objective decisions, you will more than likely live within your financial level and have better command of your income.

Controlling Cash. If you're not careful, cash has a way of disappearing. How often have you asked yourself, "Where did it all go?" Well, for openers, how about carfare, laundry, lunch, tips, entertainment, snacks, gifts, somethings, nothings?

To know where your cash went and to prevent it from going where it shouldn't, you must keep track of out-of-pocket expenditures regularly—at least once a day. If there are large discrepancies between what you think you spent and what's actually left, it's a sign that you're not as attentive to your expenditures as you should be. Good times to check cash are just after lunch and/or in the evening when the day's spending is over.

Knowing Billing Cycles. Be aware of how billing cycles work. Take, for example, routine responsibilities such as dental checkups. Suppose your dentist regularly bills on the first of the month. Schedule your appointment for the third of the month so you won't get a bill for at least three weeks.

The same approach holds true for credit purchases made in department stores. "Playing the billing cycle," one systems officer says, "is as good as getting an interest-free loan for 30 days."

Another thought: If your personal money is tight, charge on the plate that gives you the longest period of collection. This way you can pick up weeks of free money. But, keep a record of how much you have charged so you will be sure to set aside enough money to cover the bill.

Bargain Hunting. This is a foolproof way to get more value for your money. And besides, bargain hunting can be fun! Be diligent, buy out of season, use discount stores and factory outlets. Keep an eye out for warehouse and clearance sales.

Be sure to comparison shop. You can do this by actually visiting stores, or you can assemble a file of newspaper ads especially on significantly priced items (TV, stereo, furniture). Always be prepared for traditional sale periods.

January—The big month for inventory clearances. Christmas cards, wrappings, decorations on sale; also the month for White Sales on towels and bedding.

February—Washington and Lincoln's Birthday storewide sales.

March and April—After Easter storewide sales.

May—Memorial Day storewide sales.

July—Fourth of July storewide sales. Summer fashion clearances begin.

August—Another month for White Sales. A good time to start shopping for bargains in cars.

September—Labor Day specials. Watch for sales on tires and car clearances.

October—Columbus Day storewide sales.

November—Election Day and Veterans' Day storewide sales.

December—After Christmas clearances.

Saving Techniques. First, you have to have something to save, so controlling impulse spending is a "must." It's a good idea to "sleep" on the impulse to buy for a couple of days. Often the desire will fade—but your money won't.

You can also control impulse spending by setting a weekly limit for out-of-pocket expenditures. Let's say it's $5 per weekday or a total of $25 per work week. You should furnish yourself with five $5 bills at the beginning of the week. Larger or smaller bills could cause confusion. On Wednesday morning you should wake up with three $5 bills. If you have less, you have spent too much on Monday and Tuesday and should plan on cutbacks for the rest of the week. Not having more cash on hand keeps you from spending.

Tipping. Overtipping, psychologists have often said, is a sign of insecurity. It's also one of the fastest ways of putting money that should be in your pocket into someone else's pocket. On the other hand, undertipping is an insulting way to short change good service. It's better to strike a happy medium, one that is fair to everyone, including yourself.

Waiters and Waitresses—15% of the bill in better restaurants, 20% in exceptional restaurants. At a counter 10–15% is considered adequate at breakfast or lunch, 15–20% at dinner. Cocktail waiters or waitresses should get 15% (minimum 25 cents per person). Wine stewards—$1 per bottle.

Bartender—15% if you're sitting at the bar, nothing if you're sitting at a table and you're served by someone else.

Taxi Driver—25 cents minimum, usually 20% of the bill.

Airport Porter—25 to 50 cents per bag, depending on whether he loads it into the taxi or car himself, or hands it to someone else at the curb.

Red Cap (in bus terminals) — There is usually a fixed cost (25 to 35 cents) per bag, and the Red Cap is tipped on top of this, usually 25 cents.

Bellhop — 25 cents per bag.

Chambermaid — Nothing if your stay is short; $1 to $2 and up if you stay longer and/or she performs extra services.

Hotel or Apartment Door Guard — 25 cents if he hails a cab, otherwise nothing.

Ladies Room/Mens Room Attendant — 25 cents, optional unless they perform a service.

Hat Check Attendant — 25 cents per person. Sometimes a set fee.

Christmas Tipping. In many cities, it is customary to Christmas tip those who have rendered services all year long. The people you might consider for such a gratuity include your building superintendent, the door guard, elevator operator, hairdresser, regular babysitter, those who deliver the milk, newspaper, and mail, garage attendant, and cleaning help. As you can see, the list can get quite lengthy — and expensive. A rule of thumb — a Christmas tip, from $2 to $10, should be given only to those who have rendered exceptional service during the year.

Banking: The Basics

As soon as you start earning money, banking will probably become part of your life. To understand banking from the outset, study the following discussion of banking.

What Is a Commercial Bank? It's a nongovernment financial institution that provides checking accounts, savings accounts, various consumer loans (such as auto, home improvement and education) and safe-deposit facilities. It sells and redeems U.S. Savings Bonds; prepares cash payrolls for local businesses; offers mortgages on residential property; offers Christmas and other club savings accounts; issues bank credit cards, travelers checks and bank money orders; and, in many instances, provides trust services.

Who Owns a Commercial Bank? It's a corporation owned by stockholders—the public—who elect a board of directors to oversee the performance of the bank's management and professional staff.

How Does a Commercial Bank Make a Profit? Bank profits come from interest on loans and from investments the bank makes in government and private securities. Bank deposits are used, first and foremost, to make loans, for additional investments, and to pay bank operating expenses such as salaries. Since commercial banks are owned by the public, they return a portion of profits to shareholders in the form of dividends.

The Value of a Checking Account. A checking account is not only a convenient method of paying bills, it also eliminates the need to have large sums of cash on hand. It saves the expense of obtaining money orders to pay routine bills and allows you to pay bills by mail rather than taking the time and spending the money for transportation and possibly parking to pay bills with cash in person.

Special Checking Account versus Regular Checking Account

A *special checking account* is one that requires no minimum balance. However, you pay for each check that you write. The fee is usually 15 cents per check; a monthly maintenance fee may be as low as 25 cents or as high as $1.00 or more.

A *regular checking account* is designed for people who can keep a minimum balance in the account. If you maintain or exceed that balance each month there is no maintenance charge. If you fall short, then you pay maintenance fees according to your bank's fee schedule. Banks can afford to give you cost-free maintenance on a regular checking account for a very obvious reason. They are able to use your steady balance to turn a profit for their corporation. Thus, it's a good deal for the customer and the bank.

The choice of special checking account or regular must be based on your financial position. If you can't afford to keep a steady minimum balance then, of course, it's better to pay the fees that come with a special checking account.

Frequently Asked Questions About Checks

Q. If the amount of a check shown in figures is different from the amount written out, does the bank refuse to pay the check?
A. No. The bank regards the amount written out as the correct figure. If you realize after a check has left your hands that it contains an error, call your bank and stop payment.
Q. Is a check valid if it is dated on a Sunday or holiday?
A. Yes. It's not true that checks can only be dated on days when banks are open. However, a check over six months old may be rejected. In January and February it is especially important to date your checks with the correct year.
Q. Why do I have to balance the bank statement with my check book? Doesn't the bank keep my account straight?
A. The bank keeps a running daily record of the status of your account. However, the bank doesn't know what checks you have written until they are presented for payment. To avoid writing a check in an amount larger than your account balance, you must keep accurate records. If your bank statement seems to indicate a discrepancy check it promptly and notify your bank.
Q. How and when should you stop payment on a check?

A. If you write a check for an incorrect amount or wish to revoke a check written to a person or company, you may instruct your bank to refuse payment on it. To do this, call or visit your bank immediately with the check number and the payee's name and amount. If the check has not already been paid, the bank will issue a stop payment order, indicating that the check should not be paid when presented. In the meantime you will receive a form to sign and return. This will verify your stop payment request. There is a charge for this service. Ask your bank for the exact amount at the outset.

Q. How long does a stop payment continue in effect?

A. It will remain in effect for six months. If the check hasn't been presented for payment during that time, you may renew the stop payment order.

Interest Rates

Prime interest is the rate at which a commercial bank makes loans to its best and most credit-worthy business and industrial customers. The level of the prime rate is determined by how much banks have to pay for the supply of money from which they make their loans. In an inflated economy banks pay increasingly higher rates for funds, and thus, the prime rate has risen in recent years. When inflation subsides, the prime rate usually drops.

The prime rate can be considered a sort of quantity discount for large sums of borrowed money for which the borrower must have an excellent credit rating, sufficient collateral to cover a large loan, and the capacity to use the loan funds productively (such as building a new factory, providing increased goods or services, or creating additional employment opportunities).

Thus, most of us would have little reason to borrow at the prime or wholesale rate. Actually some consumer loans are issued at *less* than the prime rate. Two examples are auto and mortgage loans. Consumer loan rates, while they are generally higher than prime rates, tend to be more stable.

Interest on Savings Accounts. Because savings banks are formed essentially to provide mortgage loans, they are permitted to give slightly higher interest on savings. Keep that in mind and check out interest rates before giving your savings business to any bank. Remember, comparison shopping always works in your favor.

Always get the most for your money. At the same time remember that a savings bank, by its very nature, does not offer the range of services provided by commercial banks.

Applying for a Loan. When, or if, you apply for a loan one of the first questions you will encounter is, "Reason for loan?" The banks ask this (without fail) because the purpose of the loan may affect the type of contract, the length of time allowed for repayment, the interest rate, and even whether or not the loan should be granted.

Cosigning a Loan: What's the Liability? If the borrower defaults, the cosigner is fully liable! So don't ever be casual about backing up someone else's loan. If you do cosign, read and understand thoroughly all the terms of the loan or sales beforehand.

What's the Meaning of "Collateral?" Quite simply collateral is anything of value that a bank accepts as security against the repayment of a loan. Stocks, bonds, savings account passbooks (whose balance would represent at least the amount borrowed) and other marketable property are used as collateral.

Estates. The elementary definition of an estate is the assets and liabilities of a deceased or bankrupt person. Here we concern ourselves only with that estate as it refers to a deceased person.

Q. What is the difference between an executor and an administrator of an estate?
A. An executor is selected by the estate owner to distribute the estate according to the terms of his or her will. When there is no will, an administrator is appointed by the court to settle the estate according to the provisions of the law.
Q. What happens if the executor of a will dies while settling the estate?
A. In making out a will, you should designate an executor and name an alternate. If you name your bank as executor, this problem will not occur.
Q. What happens to the funds in a savings account when the owner of the account dies?
A. The bank will release the funds to the executor or administrator. In some circumstances, if no executor or administrator has been appointed, the bank can release some funds to a member of the family or the undertaker.
Q. What happens to the estate of a husband and wife who die at the same time (in an accident)?
A. If the wills simply left the property of each to the other, and both died simultaneously, the wills would be of no use in this situation. Thus, if you are planning marriage, your wills should be drawn to provide for this possibility, insuring a secondary distribution of your estate in accordance with your wishes.

Wills. To many people, especially those who are having the time of their lives, the subject of a will is morbid. Nevertheless, it is an important document if you are to manage all phases of your life.

There is nothing tricky about drawing up a will. Anyone who meets his or her state requirements (in most states you have to be 21 years old; in some, 18) can do it. It doesn't even require a lawyer although legal assistance is definitely recommended. The law recognizes any piece of paper that you have clearly labeled *will* and signed in the presence of two witnesses (who should not be beneficiaries) as long as you have complied with the mandatory requirements of your state. This is where the expertise and experience of a lawyer becomes a near necessity.

The legal charge for a simple will should be about $50 but this also varies.

A will is advisable even if you have only a few possessions (assets). It gives you the undisputed power to leave things to people of your own choosing. If you don't have a will your property automatically goes to your parent(s) or next of kin. If you don't want it this way, a will allows you to specify an executor other than a parent or next of kin.

When you have a will, it should be periodically reviewed with your lawyer. You may have a change of heart. Also, wills should be changed to keep up with revised tax laws.

Credit

For quite some time now we have been living in a credit-oriented society. People who don't have enough readily available cash use consumer credit to help pay for home furnishings, cars, major home appliances and equipment, clothing, vacations, remodeling, medical bills, even old debts.

Types of Consumer Credit

Short Term. There are two major categories: retail and cash services from department stores, appliance dealers, and furniture stores. Retailers offer 30 day accounts, revolving accounts, and installment plans.

Thousands of consumers also purchase goods and services with bank cards, American Express, Diner's Club and Carte Blanche cards, and oil company cards. (see section on credit cards which follows).

To use consumer credit efficiently:

1. Understand all the types and sources.
2. Use only for purposes that are consistent with income, spending plan, and long-range goals.
3. Shop for the best plan and services and the lowest terms available to meet needs.
4. Limit credit to what can be repaid comfortably.
5. Fulfill repayment responsibilities.

Long Term. This most often is synonomous with home mortgages. Although this information may not apply to you right now, it could come in handy in the years ahead.

What usually is referred to as a mortgage today is actually two documents—the mortgage itself, which pledges property as security against the loan, and a promissory note, in which the purchaser agrees to make specified payments of principal and interest for a certain number of years.

Home mortgage loans are granted by various financial institutions, namely, commercial banks, some life insurance companies, mortgage banking firms, mutual savings banks, and savings and loan associations.

There are three major types of mortgage loans: conventional, FHA insured, and VA guaranteed. Conventional loans are transactions between the borrower and a financial institution. FHA (Federal Housing Administration) loans are obtained through a financial institution but evaluated and insured by the federal government. VA (Veterans Administration) loans are granted by financial institutions but guaranteed by the government. These loans are made only to war veterans who qualify.

When you start to look for a house, you should know the current mortgage market, shop for the best terms and lowest interest rates, know what the down payment will be, and what the terms include. Talk to knowledgeable friends, consult a banker you know, and obtain legal assistance.

Establishing Credit. Is credit easy to get? It all depends upon overall credit worthiness. How is that determined? What happens when you apply for a credit account or a loan?

First, identification is required; for example, driver's license, social security card, voter's registration card, employment identification card. Second, other personal information is necessary: place of residence, period of time lived there, whether you rent or own, place of employment, type of work, length of time employed, salary, where you bank, whether you have savings and checking accounts elsewhere.

This information is requested in an interview or on an application or both, depending upon the type of credit. This credit profile will help the creditor determine whether the prospective credit user can and will pay for the credit and/or merchandise that's in question.

To obtain credit, a future user must have a regular income, a good record of paying bills on time and some financial resources (savings, automobile, life insurance, home).

A consumer's credit ratings begins the first time credit is used. It is strengthened when bills are paid promptly and regularly and when credit is used in amounts that can be safely repaid.

Why Use Credit Cards?

Convenience. Credit cards, in effect, are a ready means to obtain an unsecured loan. By establishing your credit you're able to buy things without paying cash and without putting up property in exchange for the loan. With some credit cards you can get a cash advance as well. Of course, as we have said, you must maintain a good credit rating by establishing reliability through timely payments.

Instant Credit. As a reliable credit card holder, one who pays regularly and spends within the limits established by a credit card company, you can buy things without delay.

Emergency Use. Because you do have instant credit, you're able to charge things that you need or want unexpectedly. If you run low on cash while vacationing, a credit card can bring relief. If you discover a bargain that you didn't anticipate, you can buy it.

Flexibility. The purchasing scope of credit cards has mushroomed in recent years. The bulk of credit card activity relates to retail goods, gasoline, restaurant meals and beverages, hotel and motel accommodations, and transportation. Yet there are instances of credit cards being used to purchase goods in supermarkets, pay the rent, cab fares, insurance premiums — even some political contributions have been charged!

Cash Substitute. A principal advantage of a credit card is the fact that you don't have to carry around large amounts of cash. On many occasions you will also avoid the uncomfortable need to produce all sorts of identification when you want to pay by personal check.

Ease of Payment. Credit card invoices are sent out once a month. You can pay for all purchases on any card with just one check or money order. This could save on banking charges among other things and it's just plain easier than making a lot of different payments. Credit card purchases also provide you with a permanent record of expenditures.

Three Types of Credit Cards

Bank Card. These are all-purpose cards with which you can pay for retail goods, meals, lodgings, transportation, and more, at over a million business outlets throughout the United States and the world. Usually you can get a cash advance of $50 or $100, perhaps more, from participating banks.

Bank cards set limits on how much credit you can have.

Typically it's $500 (some accounts go much higher). You won't be allowed to charge beyond your limit. Stores are required to make a phone call to their bank card center for approval of any transaction above a certain amount.

A local bank may have its imprint on your card, but there are just two major bank card companies in the country, BankAmericard and Master Charge.

Travel and Entertainment Card. These include American Express, Diners' Club, and Carte Blanche. They're honored at many restaurants, hotels and motels, retail stores, airlines, and car rentals. Some travel cards also provide a toll-free phone service to guarantee hotel and motel reservations.

Although these companies don't impose official limits on the amount of outstanding debt you can have, they keep close tabs on your payment records. If you seem to be on a spending spree or are slow in paying, you may be asked to stop using the card until your account is clear. If matters get totally out of hand, you cannot use the card altogether, a serious blow to your overall credit rating.

One-Company Cards. Here we have some variety. Most major gasoline and oil companies issue cards you can use only at their service stations, and sometimes at others. Sometimes, these cards can be used for hotels and restaurants. Many local department stores and national chain stores have their own cards. Some of these establishments accept bank or travel cards as well. There are also airline and auto rental company cards.

How to Get a Credit Card. You'll find bank card application forms at participating banks, stores, and other outlets. Travel card applications are available in restaurants and stores. One-company card applications can be found at retail stores and service station outlets.

All applications go through a credit check. Bank and gasoline cards are usually given to anyone with good credit standing, even though his or her income is relatively modest. The travel, car rental, and airline companies have stricter income standards—typically, at least $8500 a year. Individual stores and chains set their own criteria.

Credit Discrimination. In 1974, The Equal Credit Opportunity Act was passed by Congress and signed into law. This act forbids discrimination by creditors on the basis of sex or marital status and applies to all who regularly extend credit including department stores, banks, finance companies, and credit card issuers. Some of the main provisions of this act include:

1. The regulation forbids the use of sex or marital status in credit scoring systems.
2. Creditors are required to provide, at the applicant's request, the reasons for terminating or denying credit.
3. In evaluating credit worthiness, creditors may not inquire about birth control practices or childbearing capabilities or intentions.
4. Credit applicants who feel they are the victims of discrimination may file suit for actual damages and for punitive damages up to $10,000.
5. Separate accounts may not be refused to qualified applicants on the basis of sex or marital status. A married woman's credit account may now be maintained in her own name rather than that of her husband's as previously required by most creditors.
6. Terms in application forms must be neutral as to sex. Designating the titles of Mr., Mrs., Miss, or Ms. is optional.

What Do Credit Cards Cost? The travel card companies charge an annual fee of $15 or $20 but no interest on the loan. However, for something like a plane ticket you can make an extended payment arrangement for which there will be a 12% annual interest rate. Personal air travel cards charge an 18% annual rate for payments extended beyond 25 days. There are no charges on car rental cards.

You don't pay a fee for a bank card, but there is interest

if you haven't paid within a certain time — usually 25 days from the billing date. This interest ranges from 1 to $1\frac{1}{2}$% per month or a 12 to 18% annual rate. The same is true of most retail store cards. State law regulates such interest rates.

Note: Sometimes charge account bills don't arrive until long after the billing date, giving you little chance to get your payment in before interest is charged. If this happens, don't just write it off to *red tape*. Complain immediately to the company or store. If these late mailings continue, it may not be red tape at all but an unethical scheme to get interest money that you shouldn't pay. In this case contact your local office of the Federal Trade Commission (or State banking authority, for bank cards). Legislation is now pending to protect you from these unfair practices. But, until its passage, you must rely on self-protection.

Liability in Case of Loss. If your card is lost or stolen and someone else uses it, your liability stops at $50. That's the law. As a matter of fact, if you notify your credit card company in time, you won't even be liable for $50.

In any event you should take these precautions:

1. Keep a list of all cards, account numbers, names, addresses, and phone numbers of the companies. Keep the list in a place separate from your cards. It's a good idea to keep two lists, one at home and one at your place of work. If your cards are lost or stolen, contact each company immediately by phone or wire. Then follow with a letter.
2. Carry your cards separate from your wallet.
3. Keep only those cards that you intend to use. Cancel, then cut in half, those cards that you seldom if ever use or the ones that duplicate others.
4. If you have many credit cards, it might be a good idea to consider credit card insurance.

Checking up on Your Credit. Over 100,000,000 credit files now exist in this country and increasingly people are discovering that their files contain inaccurate or out-of-date information that should be corrected or removed.

Thanks to the Fair Credit Reporting Act, you can now check into your credit file to determine whether any information should be changed to improve your credit standing.

Know Your Rights. According to the Fair Credit Reporting Act, the FTC maintains (FTC Buyers Guide No. 7) that you have the following absolute rights:

1. To be told the name and address of the consumer reporting agency responsible for preparing a consumer report that was used to deny you credit, insurance, employment, or to increase the cost of credit or insurance.
2. To be told by a consumer-reporting agency the nature, substance, and sources (except investigative type sources) of the information (except medical) collected about you.
3. To take anyone of your choice with you when you visit the consumer reporting agency to check on your file.
4. To obtain all information to which you are entitled, free of charge, when you have been denied credit, insurance, or employment within 30 days of your interview. Otherwise, the reporting agency is permitted to charge a reasonable fee for giving you the information.
5. To be told who has received a consumer report on you within the preceding six months, or within the preceding two years if the report was furnished for employment purposes.
6. To have incomplete or incorrect information re-

investigated, and, if the information is found to be inaccurate or cannot be verified, to have such information removed from your file.

7. To have the agency notify those you name (at no cost to you) who have previously received the incorrect or incomplete information that this information has been deleted from your file.
8. When a dispute between you and the reporting agency about information in your file cannot be resolved, you have the right to have your version of such a dispute placed in the file and included in future consumer reports.
9. To request the reporting agency to send your version of the dispute to certain businesses for a reasonable fee.
10. To have a consumer report withheld from anyone who under the law does not have a legitimate business need for the information.
11. To sue a reporting agency for damages if it willfully or negligently violates the law and, if you are successful, you can collect attorney's fees and court costs.
12. Not to have adverse information reported after seven years. One major exception is bankruptcy, which may be reported for 14 years.
13. To be notified by a business that it is seeking information about you which would constitute an "Investigative Consumer Report."
14. To request from the business that ordered an investigative report more information about the nature and scope of the investigation.
15. To discover the nature and substance (but not the source) of the information that was collected for an "Investigative Consumer Report."

On the other hand, the Fair Credit Reporting Act does not:

1. Give you the right to request a report on yourself from the consumer reporting agency.
2. Give you the right, when you visit the agency, to receive a copy of or to physically handle your file.
3. Compel anyone to do business with an individual consumer.
4. Apply when you request commercial (as distinguished from consumer) credit or business insurance.
5. Authorize any federal agency to intervene on behalf of an individual consumer.

How to Locate Your Local Credit Bureau (Agency). Once you have established credit, whether it be good or bad, you can be nearly certain that there's a credit profile bearing your name at your local Credit Bureau or Agency. The identity of that particular bureau is a carefully guarded secret of the credit bureau trade association: Associated Credit Bureaus, Houston, Texas. However, you can locate your local Credit Bureau on your own as follows:

1. Look in the yellow pages of your telephone book under CREDIT BUREAUS or CREDIT REPORTING AGENCIES. Now look for one of the following prefixes "THE CREDIT BUREAU OF" (Greater New York, Inc.) or "THE CREDIT BUREAU OF" (Milwaukee, Inc.). Also be alert for the following key names—"CREDIT REPORTS, INC." and "CREDIT INFORMATION, INC. You may inquire by telephone whether your credit file is there.
2. Ask any local bank officer where your credit file may be located. If this information still eludes you, call your local Better Business Bureau or nearest Federal Trade Commission office.
3. If you are still unable to find your local Credit Bureau write Credit Watchers, Inc., 2 Penn Plaza,

New York 10001. They'll surely have the right name for you.

A Checklist to Keep Handy. If you decide to visit a Credit Bureau to check on your file here is a helpful checklist.

Did you:

1. Learn the nature and substance of all the information in your file?
2. Find out the names of each of the businesses (or other sources) that supplied information on you to the reporting agency?
3. Learn the names of everyone who received reports on you within the past six months (or the last two years if the reports were for employment purposes)?
4. Request the agency to reinvestigate and correct or delete information that was found to be inaccurate, incomplete, or obsolete?
5. Follow up to determine the results of the reinvestigation?
6. Ask the agency, at no cost to you, to notify those you name who received reports within the past six months (two years if for employment purposes) that certain information was deleted?
7. Follow up to make sure that those named by you did in fact receive notices from the consumer bureau or reporting agency?
8. Demand that your version of the facts be placed in your file if the reinvestigation did not settle the dispute?
9. Request the agency (if you are willing to pay a reasonable fee) to send your statement of the dispute to those you name who received reports containing the disputed information within the past six months (two years if received for employment purposes)?

Some Credit Do's and Don't's. The Department of Consumer Affairs for the City of New York has what it calls "some hard facts on 'easy' credit." Gutsy and to the point, they're good closing thoughts on the subject of credit.

Do

- shop for credit as carefully as you do for merchandise. Compare! The price of credit varies as much as the price of goods.
- find out the different sources of available credit. Compare the costs of borrowing from banks, credit unions, finance companies with the costs of installment buying.
- consider the possibility of trying to get a loan for the entire purchase.
- study the price tag on merchandise you're planning to buy in installments. It must tell you the interest rate in % and the finance charge in $.
- make as large a down payment as possible if you do buy on the installment plan. Make your payments as large as you can to pay back as fast as you can.
- look for the Notice to the Buyer before you sign a contract:
    1) Do not sign this agreement before you read it, or if it contains any blank spaces.
    2) You are entitled to a complete copy of this agreement.
- read the contract carefully.
- demand a copy of the signed contract. Take it with you, and keep it in a safe place.
- know what the penalties are if you can't make your payments.
- protect yourself against unlawful harrassment by creditors. They are not allowed to threaten action which they have no legal right to take.
- inform the bank or finance company acting as collection agents if you have a justified dispute with a home im-

provement contractor and want to suspend your payments.
- ► know that if a lawsuit is brought against you for default of payments, it must be brought in the county *you* live in, or in the county where the purchase was made.
- ► be sure that you get your charge account statement in the mail 15 days before any finance charges take effect, so that you have time to pay your bill in full, if this is your practice.

Don't

- ► believe there is any "easy credit." Only getting it may be easy—paying it back is always hard.
- ► buy on installment credit until you have looked into all the other possibilities.
- ► forget that for cash you can buy at a discount house.
- ► forget that the law demands that you have this information so that you know the total price you'll end up paying.
- ► be misled into thinking that many small payments will be easier. They will cost you more in the long run.
- ► be rushed into signing anything. If the bargain won't be there tomorrow, maybe you shouldn't grab it today.
- ► sign if there are any blank spaces that could be filled in later.
- ► misplace your contract. Without it, you'll have a tough time if any problems arise.
- ► despair! In an emergency you may be able to work out an arrangement with the seller or holder of the contract.
- ► be intimidated. Creditors are not permitted to garnishee your wages, or contact your boss *unless* there is a court judgment against you.
- ► let them tell you that they are not responsible for the contractor they financed. A new law says they are.
- ► believe that the seller can arbitrarily pick a distant court, just to make it hard for you to appear.

> pay a penalty in interest charges because the store failed to send its bill on time. It's their fault—not yours!

Insurance

Life. People buy life insurance for a number of reasons. The main one is to provide financial protection for those who rely on them for some or all of their support. Then, too, cash values or guaranteed funds as you will see can be useful in middle or old age.

In business, principals of corporations or partnerships often have life insurance policies naming each other as beneficiaries. This arrangement provides a surviving principal or principals with sufficient funds to buy the other partner's interest from the heirs.

For those who may have to accumulate a debt to obtain education, there are policies to help make certain that the indebtedness will be paid.

Whatever the reasons, you should be familiar with the different types of life insurance policies available today. There are four basic kinds.

Straight Life Policy. This type offers protection for an entire lifetime. The premium remains the same each year. In addition this policy builds a cash value which you can redeem when you reach a specified age.

Limited Payment Life Policy. This one protects for life but the premiums are concentrated into a specified number of years—usually 10, 20, or 30 years. Or, you may pay premiums until a certain age, usually 60 or 65 years. The premium is higher than for a straight life policy for the same amount because the period of payments is shorter. However, the cash value grows faster.

Endowment Policies. These enable you to accumulate a sum of money which becomes available to *you* at a certain date. Meanwhile, there is insurance protection for the full amount to those who depend on you, should you die before the end of the policy period. Endowments build the largest cash values of any type of life insurance policy.

Term Insurance Policies. They provide life insurance coverage for a given period of time, which can be 5, 10, 15, or 20 years or to age 65. Some term insurance policies are renewable at the end of the term, but the premium will be higher each time it is renewed. Most term insurance policies do not accumulate cash values.

Some policies combine the features of two types of insurance to meet special needs. There are *family income plans* that combine life and term insurance to provide greater family protection at low cost while children are young.

Retirement Income Policy. This policy combines life insurance with provision for a lifetime income. It guarantees income for a beneficiary before that income begins.

Annuities. Annuities are sold by life insurance companies but they are not life insurance. Where the primary purpose of life insurance is to protect dependents, an annuity is designed to provide the owner with a guaranteed retirement income for life.

There are two kinds of annuities: *straight life* and *refund*. With the straight life annuity, payments stop when the owner dies. Refund annuity payments are made to a beneficiary if the owner dies before receiving the amount paid into the annuity. Straight life annuities cost less than comparable refund annuities but pay a large income since they are on the life of one person only.

Tax-shelter annuities are a relatively recent development for people employed in certain charitable, educational, and religious organizations. Up to a given level, a portion of one's salary allocated to these annuities is not taxable as current income. The effect is to lower income taxes during the earning years.

Another new development is the *variable annuity*. As with the regular annuity, it provides a monthly income for life. However, the funds behind the variable annuity are invested in common stocks. Thus, retirement benefits may vary from month to month although they will not fall below a given amount. Most variable annuities are available on a group basis through employers, but some life insurance companies are now making these available to individuals.

To some, perhaps many people, insurance terminology is awesome, even uncomprehensible. To avoid "small print-ities," a phobia that may stay with you forever if you're not careful, you should select an insurance company and agent that inspire confidence and make you feel comfortable. Ask for explanations of everything you don't understand. Don't agree to any policy until you fully understand it and are completely satisfied with its provisions.

Health. Accidents and illness are two unpredictable possibilities in your future. You don't like to think about them but you should.

So, most people prepare themselves by having health insurance coverage. If you've ever had to pay a medical bill without the aid of health insurance you know how wise it is to be covered.

There are six kinds:

1. *Hospital expense insurance* helps pay for hospital room and board, routine nursing care, minor medical supplies, and related services.
2. *Surgical expense insurance* helps pay for the cost of operations.
3. *Physician's expense insurance* helps pay for in-hospital visits by a doctor and, depending on the policy, for home and office visits.
4. *Major medical expense insurance* helps pay bills for

serious or prolonged illness or injury in and out of hospital.
5. *Dental expense insurance* helps pay for normal dental care and, depending on the policy, dentures, orthodontics, and annual checkups.
6. *Disability income insurance* helps to replace earnings you lose when you are unable to work because of illness or injury.

Hospital, surgical, and physicians' expense insurance provide basic coverage. Major medical and disability income coverage provide more extensive benefits.

If you work full-time, you probably have some basic protection under a group plan through an insurance company, Blue Cross, Blue Shield, or some other type of insuring organization. Many group plans also include major medical insurance. Maximum benefits of such protection usually range from $20,000 to $100,000 or more and help pay for almost every type of care and treatment prescribed by a physician, both in the hospital and at home.

Most major medical insurance policies have a "deductible" feature which means that you pay bills up to a certain amount before the insurance company takes over. The deductible amount can range from $50 to $1,000. The higher the deductible amount, the lower the cost of the insurance.

Dental expense insurance is growing more popular. It is usually available on a group basis.

Disability insurance provides continuing income that will help pay the bills that never seem to stop—rent, food, electricity—when your salary stops.

The other type of insurance, auto insurance, that you may be anticipating at this point, is covered in Chapter 8.

Investments

Once you have planned for basic protection needs, regular living requirements, and money for emergencies, you may want to invest in stocks, bonds, and other securities to earn additional capital, interest, or dividends.

No single investment offers the utopian combination of maximum safety, steady income, high return, and potential growth. Generally speaking, the higher the return, or the higher the growth potential, the greater the risk to your money.

Securities. The three most common types of securities for individual investment are common stocks, preferred stocks, and bonds.

Common and Preferred Stocks

Common stock is the number one security, basic to all corporate business and to our whole free enterprise system. When you buy a company's common stock, you become a stockholder in that company. In effect you're a part owner. What part you own depends on how many shares you own in relationship to the total number of shares that exist.

You invest in a certain company because you think it makes a good product and it is likely to make money. If *it* does, then *you* stand to make money. This can happen through the payment of dividends and/or through the increase in the market value of the stock.

Common stock is considered riskier than preferred stock but it does offer more favorable growth potential. In other words, common stock is subject to greater fluctuation than preferred stock.

As the name implies, *preferred stock* assures preferential treatment for its owner. It assures that the owner has a prior claim on all assets after all debts have been taken care of, should it ever be necessary to liquidate the company. It also accords a priority in the payment of dividends. On the other hand, as we said, the price usually doesn't fluctuate as much as common stock. So, while a preferred stockholder might not enjoy dramatic increases, he or she is not as vulnerable to sharp decreases. Thus, it provides a more steady income security than do common stocks.

Bonds. Essentially, a bond is an I.O.U. Bonds are issued by corporations, the U.S. Government, and municipalities. A bond is held by the lender as proof that he has loaned a specified amount of money. You invest in bonds not for growth potential but for steady income in the form of interest payments. Therein is the difference between stocks and bonds. A stockholder as a part owner in a company expects to collect dividends and can further profit when the market value of his stock goes up. The person who buys a company's bonds is a creditor, not a part owner, and expects to receive a *fixed* return on his investment (although interest rates on some bonds can fluctuate). So you can see that bonds are a more conservative, less risky investment than stocks.

Should you buy bonds or maintain a savings account? It's a good question that should be asked of a banker or stock broker. Some bonds have often paid higher interest than savings, but it's not always that simple. So, investigate it thoroughly. For one thing there are different types of bonds: corporate, long term issues or treasury bonds, treasury bills with maturities as short as 91 days, certificates ranging up to a year, notes that may run up to seven years, savings bonds (Series E and H) which are never traded in any market and never suffer any fluctuation in interest payment.

The Trading of Stock. A stock exchange is simply a marketplace where people buy and sell stocks every day through authorized agents or brokers.

The price of a stock is established when buyers compete with other buyers for the lowest price. It's more or less like an auction where bidder and seller conclude a transaction at a price that is mutually the best that both could get at that moment.

What Does It Cost to Buy Stocks? Generally, the commission charged on stock transactions averages out to about 1%. However, it could be as high as 6% if the order is for less than $100 worth of securities. There is a standard schedule of minimum commission rates for the purchase and sale of stocks, but it can change from time to time with the approval of the Securities and Exchange Commission. If you have a large order, you should comparison shop commission costs. Some brokers may charge less than others.

Finding and Dealing with a Broker. If you don't know the name of a broker, one of your friends or associates might. Otherwise, look in the financial section of your daily newspaper. Decide which firm seems to have the policy you like and the service you need. Then visit your choice. Just drop in; you don't need any formal introduction.

Some consumers are awed by the brokerage business. Actually, it's not high hat at all. So don't be shy. And don't be defensive if your potential investment is only several hundred dollars. Small investors are being encouraged more than ever.

When you introduce yourself and your finances to a broker, be candid. The more you tell the broker about your finances — your income, your expenses, your savings, your insurance, your obligations like a mortgage or tuition payments — the better he or she will be able to plan an investment program that is suited to you as an individual.

Listed and Over-the-Counter Stocks. There are about 3,000 securities being traded on the registered stock exchanges today. That seems like a lot until you realize that there are some 50,000 unlisted securities also available!

To be listed on a registered stock exchange, a company must meet certain qualifications. There are many companies which cannot meet these requirements but they are sanctioned by the Securities and Exchange Commission (SEC) to issue stock and they become part of the over-the-counter market. Companies which do meet the requirements may choose not to be listed with a stock exchange and elect the over-the-counter method of selling, as well. In other words, over-the-counter stocks are not traded on the floor of an exchange but rather through a massive network of telephone and teletype wires that link together thousands of securities firms in the United States and abroad.

The chief attraction of the over-the-counter market is that you might find a future Xerox or IBM. There's an air of speculation about over-the-counter investments. Yet there are securities of some very solid companies — for instance, banks, life insurance and fire and casualty insurance companies — being traded every day on over-the-counter basis. So don't form stereotypes until you've checked out the securities that are recommended to you by a broker or that are of particular interest to you.

Taxes

Preparing Your Tax Return. On January 1st every year the countdown for tax returns begins. Invariably, thousands of people wait until the last minute. Some even apply for special extensions. It's not a smart habit, especially if you're preparing your own return as opposed to using an accountant because you may overlook something important in the rush. Something important like a legal deduction that might save you some money.

Forms. 1040A, commonly referred to as the short form, is recommended by the Internal Revenue Service for taxpayers who have earned less than $10,000 and have no unusual tax deductions. With it comes an automatic 15% deduction for the filing taxpayer.

If your income is about $10,000 and you have some sizeable deductions, e.g. bad debts, heavy medical expenses, real estate sales losses, large contributions, certain business expenses that you paid with personal funds, then by all means file a long form or *1040*. There are also lots of Supplemental Treasury forms like Form 2106 (Statement of Employee Business Expenses) and Form 2120 (Multiple Support Declaration). But let's just stick with 1040.

Before putting pencil to paper, gather all documents that will have bearing on your return. Start with your W-2 form (or forms if you had more than one employer during the taxable year). You should have two copies of each. Copy B is the one you send in with your return.

Check the list of permissible deductions that comes with form 1040 and make sure you're not overlooking anything.

Read all instructions carefully, then have a dry run. In other words, make out one return in pencil, look it over, double check your figures, use it as a worksheet. When you're completely satisfied with your worksheet, transcribe your figures onto a final form, the one that you will actually send to the Internal Revenue Service.

Who Must File? According to law, citizens and residents of the United States must file returns according to these tests:

If you are:	And your gross income is at least:
Single	$2,050
Single, 65 or older	2,800
Married	2,800
Married, one spouse is 65 or older	3,550
Married, both spouses are 65 or older	4,300

If you are:	And your gross income is at least:
Married, not eligible to file a joint return	750
Dependent of your parent who may claim you as an exemption but you have investment income of any amount	750

Frequently Asked Questions about Taxes

Q. What is F.I.C.A. tax?
A. It's Social Security tax. The maximum amount to be paid each year by an employer may change from year to year. In any one year, it's possible that an individual who has worked for more than one employer might have paid more than the maximum. Add up F.I.C.A. deductions from all W-2 forms. If the total exceeds the maximum for the year claim a refund or credit.
Q. If you've had your tax return for the previous year prepared by a professional can you deduct the expense this year?
A. Yes. If you itemize your deductions.
Q. Will the IRS still figure your tax on request?
A. Yes, if your adjusted gross income is $20,000 *or less* and it came only from wages, salary and tips, dividends, interest, pensions and annuities; if you claim the standard deduction; and if you file by the due date. The IRS will compute your taxes, regardless of the amount of your income, if you file by the due date on short form 1040A, and your income came only from wages, salary and tips, dividends and interest.
Q. Is it true that a student can be exempt from income tax withholding?
A. Yes. Students and other individuals are exempt from tax withholding if they did not owe tax last year, expect

to owe none in the current year and have filed a Withholding Exemption Certificate (Form W-4E) with their employers.

Q. Is it possible to reduce the amount of tax withheld from your pay?

A. Yes. In addition to claiming all exemptions to which you are entitled you may qualify for the special withholding allowance. Incidentally, if you are afraid that you will owe money at the end of the taxable year and can't bear to face that possibility, you can always have *more* tax withheld from your pay by claiming zero dependents. Some people who have had difficulties managing their money have tried this successfully. You get less money from week to week. But at the end of the year you may very well wind up with a refund rather than owing the government money.

Q. Are scholarships taxable?

A. If you receive a scholarship or fellowship grant, you may exclude all or part of that amount from your gross income, depending upon whether or not you are a degree candidate. However, a scholarship that is compensation for past or future services or primarily for the grantor's benefit is not excluded from gross income.

Q. When should you report interest earned on Series E Savings Bonds?

A. Only when the bonds mature or you cash them—whichever is earlier.

Q. What tests must be met for a taxpayer to claim a person as a dependent?

A. All five of the following tests must be fulfilled:
1. You must furnish over half of the dependent's total support during the calendar year.
2. If the person's gross income is $750 or more, you may not claim him or her as a dependent unless he or she is less than 19 years old at the end of the year or a full-time student during some part of each of five months of the year.

3. The person must be a member of your household and live with you for the entire year or he or she must be closely related to you.
4. In most cases, he or she must be a U.S. citizen or resident.
5. The person must not file a joint return, unless one is not due but was filed merely to obtain a refund.

Q. Must every taxpayer who is eligible for the short form (1040A) use it?
A. No. It's always optional.
Q. If you have to pay for transportation to a doctor's office or a hospital, is this deductible?
A. Yes. You may deduct bus, train, air, and taxi fares as well as ambulance costs. You may deduct gas, oil, tolls, parking fees.
Q. Is the cost of birth control pills deductible?
A. Yes, if the pills are prescribed by a physician. Add this to your other medical expenses. Your total medical expenses presently are deductible only to the extent they exceed 3% of your income.
Q. Must you use the tables in the IRS tax forms package to compute a sales tax deduction?
A. Using the table is optional. If you don't, be sure to keep records of actual sales tax.
Q. Can you deduct bank credit card and oil credit card finance charges?
A. Yes. They're deductible as interest and so are charges levied by retail stores on customers' revolving charge accounts and designated finance charges.
Q. Are there any upper limits on how much you can deduct as a charitable contribution?
A. In general, contributions to most charities such as churches, educational organizations, and hospitals, may be deducted up to 50% of your adjusted gross income. Contributions, like all deductions, should be supported by evidence (e.g. cancelled checks) of the donation in case of an audit.

Tax Return Tips

1. Before you file have someone else check your return for arithmetic goofs. You could avoid a 6% annual interest charge—and possible penalties. Another idea is to take your return to an office, where you have access to an adding machine or calculator and double check your addition by machine.
2. If you can't pay all the tax owed when it's due, file anyway and work out payments with the IRS. You may pay some penalty but you're not in criminal violation. And don't fall into the trap of not filing one year because you failed to file the previous year. If you have done this already, then make a voluntary disclosure of tax evasion. It's the unofficial policy of the IRS to allow the person to make amends without fear of prosecution. Before a tax disclosure, you should contact a good tax attorney.
3. If you are to meet with IRS representatives over a tax question or discrepancy, don't get unnecessarily uptight about the meeting. If you are pleasant and candid, you'll receive courteous, fair treatment.
4. If you are audited, don't panic. An audit doesn't automatically mean you'll owe more taxes. The IRS is just asking you to prove that you filed your return correctly. Occasionally people who have been audited have actually discovered that they're entitled to a refund.

Legalities

Finding a Good Lawyer. Somewhere along the way, sooner or later in your life, you will need the services of a lawyer. We have already mentioned the advisability of making out a will. When you buy a house, you have to close the deal and that requires the expertise and services of a lawyer. You may find yourself in a position where you will have to make a claim for damages against another party, or someone may make a claim against you.

Getting the right lawyer is not simply a matter of picking a person or firm that has all the right credentials and knows all the legal tricks. Legal matters are usually very personal. To represent you properly a lawyer must know a lot about you in relation to the action at hand. Very often this opens up rather intimate segments of your life, so you must feel comfortable with your lawyer. If your lawyer expresses understanding and sympathy or interest in your particular case, the chemistry is right. If you are handled impersonally or treated as though you and your case are not very important, that's a warning signal to switch attorneys.

When you're searching for a lawyer it's good to tap as many sources as you can for a recommendation. Very often the source will be an indication of the type of lawyer who's being recommended.

The ideal lawyer should offer a mixture of specialties: good negotiator, litigator, tax expert, and maybe even marital counselor. So, with this in mind, ask friends you respect and admire, your doctor, even a respected religious leader.

If, after the first consultation with a lawyer, you believe you've made a mistake, do the wisest thing: pay the consultation fee (it could range from $0 to $100) and find a replacement. In the long run it's worth the expense to be rid of an attorney who does not suit your qualifications or standards. Find out ahead of time if the lawyer charges a fee for the first consultation.

How to Sue in the People's Court. Most people have heard of the Small Claims Court (almost all states have one). But the majority don't investigate its advantages, or else they think it's not for them. It's for the people and provides a simple, fast, and practically free way to reclaim at least part of your losses.

To start proceedings it's best to go to the office of the

Small Claims Clerk (for address, look in the telephone book under state or city courts or call your local Bar Association). You'll be told whether or not your case falls within the jurisdiction of the Small Claims Court. If it does, you must limit your claim to the maximum set by each state — the amount can vary from $50 to $500. If you're not 21, you must take along a parent or legal guardian.

You then file a claim which names the person you are suing and the reason for the suit. A small filing fee is charged.

The clerk will set a trial date and notify the defendant. The hearing will be held before a judge or a lawyer acting as arbitrator; there is usually no jury. Remember to bring any proof or witnesses to support your case.

Legal Aid Society. If you cannot afford a lawyer but need representation, each state has a Legal Aid Society which will appoint a lawyer to represent you if you meet the following requirements:

1. You cannot have more than $300 in the bank.
2. You cannot have ownership of property, stocks, or bonds.
3. If you are single, you cannot gross more than $85 a week. If you are married you cannot gross more than $100 per week.

Power of Attorney. A situation may arise during which you have urgent personal affairs to attend but, because of sickness, absence, or other reason, you are unable to handle things yourself. You may need to ask someone else to take care of these affairs for you. If legal or financial matters are involved, it might be necessary for this person to have power of attorney to act for you.

Full power may be granted, or the authority may be limited to certain functions such as making bank deposits and withdrawals from a checking account.

Financial and Legal Nitty Gritty ◄ 153

In any event, power of attorney is a very serious matter and must be given a great deal of thought. A lawyer will be able to advise you if there is any real need for you to take this step.

Keeping Important Documents and Papers. As you become more involved with life, you will no doubt accumulate papers and documents that have significance and value. If they are not judiciously filed in a central location, they have a way of disappearing. Once they do, they will be difficult to replace. Here is a chart that will help you set up a system for handling such papers.

In this age of photocopies, it's a good idea and very easy to keep a copy of your important documents at home while the originals that deserve greater security are snugly stored in a safe deposit box at the bank. The reverse holds true, too. If you must have your original document at home, stash a photocopy at the bank.

Document	Keep in Safe Deposit Box	Keep at Home
Birth and death certificates	X	
Marriage license	X	
Adoption papers	X	
Divorce agreements	X	
Citizenship papers	X	
Military service records	X	
Passport		X
Diplomas		X
Social security card		X
Deeds and title papers to property	X	

Document	Keep in Safe Deposit Box	Keep at Home
Records of mortgage payments, repairs and improvements, purchase price, closing costs, and selling costs	X	
Titles, bills of sale, payment records for auto	X	
Savings certificates and passbooks	X	
Records of stocks		X
Records of bonds		X
Records of pension or profit sharing plans		X
Records of savings accounts		X
Insurance policies and records	X	
Income tax returns (also records of deductible expenses with receipts, records of income, records of payments)		X
List of credit cards and numbers		X
Canceled checks		X
List of checking accounts and account numbers		X

SOCIAL LIFE

The Art of Entertaining

Although spontaneity is always one of life's pleasant surprises, a successful party is more a matter of thoughtfulness and planning than mere circumstance.

A good host or hostess is both a director and producer. When you realize this responsibility and enjoy the prospects, your party preparations are off to a good start.

Think of Your Guests First. You should begin by considering the most important element of the party—the guests themselves. The best food and drink cannot save a gathering that has bad social chemistry.

If you are bringing together people who already have enjoyed each other's company your guest list requires no analysis whatsoever. On the other hand, if some of your guests are new to one another indulge in a little constructive psychology. Here are some questions to ask yourself.

Q. Will the interests and backgrounds of your guests make for a good mixture?

One of the greatest social sins is to be a bore. Expanding on that a bit, the easiest way to have an utterly disastrous party is to convene people who can't or won't communicate with each other. When this happens your party will ultimately if not quickly splinter into tiny, isolated groups. Individual couples may retreat within themselves. Under other circumstances two-people togetherness is beautiful. But when you have a party you must remember that you are assembling a community and the harmony of that group is your responsibility.

Q. How can you avoid incompatibility at a party?

If your guests are meeting for the first time you can't predict exactly how they will mix. But you can build in some safeguards. For example, you shouldn't overload your party with one interest group which might automatically band together in conversation, excluding — exiling — others who are in attendance. People meeting for the first time probe each other in search of rapport, a common interest or activity. Naturally when they find it they explore it. Thus, if twelve of sixteen people come from the same business or background they will utilize this common interest to communicate. Soon the four remaining guests will become outsiders. They may strive to penetrate the larger circle by listening or asking questions. But what about their thoughts and opinions? If they can't, by extraordinary command, express themselves, the party becomes a fidgety waste of time for them. And despite whatever sense of defeat they may feel it is really you who have failed them.

Conclusion: Try your best to have a balanced diet of people at your party. When there isn't one predominant group, a lot of good things can happen. There is a warmth about free conversational exchange. And often there is mutual enlightenment, compliments of a thoughtful host or hostess who has taken the time to mix the right chemicals.

The Right Atmosphere. People create auras, give off *vibes.* Other people sense them and a mood is established. When you're giving a party *your* aura is the one that counts the most. It's not that you're more important in life than your guests. The fact is that it's your place and your party and guests who accept these conditions put themselves in your hands for a certain amount of time. So, once again we're talking about being mindful of your central role and all that goes with it.

It is your responsibility to be as cordial and charming and relaxed as possible. Hopefully, this comes naturally since you are probably giving the party to be with your friends.

Of course, there are times when you may be tense from daily, unexpected pressures; from a sudden disagreement with a friend, relative, or roommate on the day of your party. Only if it is quite serious or too unshakable should you cancel your party at the last minute. Otherwise bite your lip, put the problem aside at least temporarily, and plunge ahead. Very often the charm which you must summon at first will soon begin to flow naturally. Tensions may very well disappear for good as you begin to enjoy your own party and its friendship. No matter, the point here is that you owe it to yourself and your guests to give them the best of you, not the worst.

Some people tend to get on edge before a party. It's understandable, especially if you haven't entertained often. Is everything going to be perfect? Well, if you've planned properly (more to come on this) chances are things will go very well. Perfection? Sure you should strive for it. But don't come apart if some details fail to follow your pre-party script. Just relax. By all means, don't compensate for the jitters by not being yourself. Putting on airs is a lot different than creating an aura. And to worthwhile guests it's as transparent as a pane of glass on a clear day.

So, as a host or hostess, always remember and apply one of the most vital truths of independent life—you're never better than when you're yourself. Don't get hung up on stereotypes. Not every successful host or hostess needs to have the flamboyance of "Auntie Mame." If you're extroverted that's fine. But those with quieter personalities can be good hosts and hostesses, too. What's indispensable in the make-up of a good host or hostess is the ability to be considerate about guests (before and during the party) and responsive to them within the context of the social environment that you've created. The criterion is to enjoy your guests and have your guests enjoy you and appreciate your efforts.

Planning Ahead For A Dinner Party. The party that's planned perfectly is the one that functions without anyone being conscious of all the planning. The different phases of a party should flow into each other effortlessly. The host or hostess should never appear to be strained. And here's an important, and tricky, point: the one who's in charge of cooking or preparing the food should never *get lost* in the kitchen.

This can be accomplished by planning a menu that requires a minimum amount of preparation time after the guests arrive.

Here are some rules for this kind of planning:

1. Simple, well-cooked meals with which the cook is familiar are preferable to experimental recipes. If you want to whip up something new, whether it be an appetizer, entrée or dessert, prepare it for yourself at least once before your party. If it turns out well and you're confident that you can repeat it without a hitch then you can include it in your party menu with the assurance that it won't cause a crisis.
2. Dishes that can be cooked ahead of time and be either frozen or refrigerated until needed are a great convenience.

3. Menu and marketing lists should be written out well in advance; your supply of staples should be checked as well as the needs of the specific menu. Marketing should be done at least one day in advance to avoid last minute scrambles for hard to find items.
4. Plan menus which do not complicate either the use of the oven or refrigerator storage. All foods to be cooked in the oven should require the same oven temperature. There should be ample space in the refrigerator to accommodate all cold dishes.
5. Avoid repetition of foods within the same meal. Thus, if fish is the appetizer do not use it as the main dish, too.
6. Maintain a balance between firm and soft foods.
7. Do not serve too many starches or too much of one foodstuff.
8. Avoid too many strong flavors—flavors should harmonize or contrast, but not compete. Include something sweet and something tart, something hot and something cold in every meal. Try to use colorful foods in every meal for visual appeal and excitement.
9. Do as much as possible in advance: your table can be set; raw vegetables and salad greens can be washed and prepared hours before.
10. Make a timetable to determine your cooking order. Start with the dish that takes the longest, then the next longest, and so on. This kind of timetable will allow you to serve each element properly cooked and at the proper time. Be sure serving utensils and platters are ready to use.

Seating Arrangements. Host and hostess should be seated at opposite ends of the table. (Academic if you're entertaining by yourself). We suggest that the individual who's mostly responsible for the preparation of the meal be seated at the end nearest to the kitchen. This will save steps and allow the person at the controls to be in complete control.

Arrange your guests keeping their interests and tastes in mind. Try to place together those who will find one another interesting and congenial. Usually you alternate men and women. Some people prefer to separate wives and husbands. That's up to you and your guests. Some couples may be more comfortable seated together. The best seating arrangement is the one that's the most enjoyable for everyone.

Linens and Decorations. A tablecloth should be spread so that the middle crease is up and it divides the table exactly in half with the edges hanging evenly all around the table. Placemats may be used instead of a tablecloth. It's a matter of personal taste.

If you have a center decoration on your table, make sure that it doesn't obstruct anyone's view. Candles placed at each side of the centerpiece can add a touch of formality or intimacy. But they're probably too formal for luncheons or brunches.

Set the table as neatly and attractively as possible. Avoid crowding.

Sit-Down Dinner versus the Buffet. Both types of parties are enjoyable. Obviously a sit-down dinner (luncheon or brunch) has definite space requirements. You can't invite more guests than your dining table will accommodate. A serve-yourself buffet is made to order for larger groups and is much more informal. Just make sure that each guest has a comfortable place to sit and a sturdy surface for his or her plate and glass. No one should have to balance a sagging or slippery plate and a handful of silverware for the sake of informality.

Ideally use a dining room table. If that's not practical or large enough for everyone, set up card tables or provide sturdy lap trays. Eating while sitting on the floor is okay if you have a low table. If you don't, guests probably will place their glasses on the floor and inevitably some will be knocked over by the traffic. This brings us to another point. Even though a buffet is versatile for serving larger groups, don't invite more guests than your home can accommodate comfortably. Parties that are too crowded are more a sign of your inconsideration than your popularity.

The Typical Buffet Setting. A long narrow table, placed against one wall and covered with an appropriate cloth, is particularly convenient for buffet service. However, a round, square, or oblong table will do, too.

Have plates available at one end of the table and then the main dish and accompaniments in the order in which you wish your guests to serve themselves. The traffic should move in one direction. It is customary to avoid food that requires the use of a knife, although poultry, ham and other meats are often served. Dessert and coffee can be served from a separate table or a sideboard.

Brunch. The popularity of the weekend brunch has been growing rapidly because it offers great informality and a distinctive kind of relaxation. A brunch is more of a celebration than breakfast. First of all, you can serve elements of breakfast and lunch at the meal, which means the menu has all sorts of built-in possibilities with many opportunities for surprises. Secondly, it doesn't have the time restrictions of a weekday lunch which must be terminated at a prescribed hour so that you can resume your business or educational duties. And since the weekend brunch is strictly a leisure time activity you have the latitude of serving beverages other than traditional coffee, tea, milk, and juices.

There are all sorts of foodstuffs at your disposal. Anything from scrambled eggs to blintzes. From Eggs Benedict to French Toast. For best results offer elements from brunches that have pleased you in the past. Or consult one of the many cookbooks on the subject.

The Cocktail Party. When you serve hors d'oeuvres before a dinner party, a great variety and quantity is not at all necessary. On the contrary, if you overload your guests with hors d'oeuvres, dinner will be anticlimatic. Some hosts and hostesses who serve more than one drink before dinner quite honestly offer hors d'oeuvres purely to counterbalance the effect that alcohol, by itself, may have upon their guests. In contrast, hors d'oeuvres are a much more important element at a cocktail party simply because no other food is to be provided. Thus, you should plan quantities so that there are five or six "pieces" for each guest.

Hot hors d'oeuvres should not be attempted unless they can be served piping hot. Tiny, attractive canapes are much safer. If you're on a very tight budget even bowls of nuts and potato chips or a simple dip will suffice.

When it comes to drinks, like always, consider your guests. If you know the preferences of certain guests you should do your best to have those ingredients on hand. Also be supplied with one or more non-alcoholic beverages. These include fruit juices, soft drinks, tea or coffee. Without these alternatives available you are, in effect, punishing non-drinkers — and that's an unforgiveable form of social discrimination.

In recent years wine has become one of America's favorite alcoholic beverages. So we suggest that you have some on hand. An inexpensive jug or two of domestic wine would be fine.

Selecting and Serving Wine. There are three basic kinds of wine: natural, sparkling, and fortified.

Natural wine is made by fermenting the juice of freshly squeezed grapes. As the name indicates, this is a totally natural process and it produces either a red, white or pink wine that is mild in flavor, moderate in alcoholic strength (about 9 to 14 percent alcohol by volume). Natural wine is often referred to as table wine since it is generally consumed with food.

Sparkling wine is made by bottling the wine before the fermentation is quite finished so that some of the natural carbon dioxide is trapped in the bottle. This technique creates bubbles. The best known sparkling wine is Champagne.

Fortified wines are made by adding brandy. The object is to make a sweeter wine and the addition of brandy increases the alcohol content to 15 to 21% by volume. Sherry and Port are two of the better known fortified wines.

The following chart will help you select the right wine to go with the food that you're serving.

WINE AND FOOD CHART

Wine Classification	*Basic Types*	*Wine and Food Combinations*
Apperitifs	Sherry (dry) Vermouth	Serve before meals chilled. Good with hors d'oeuvres.
White	Chablis (Burgundy) Sauterne Bordeaux White Rhine wine	Serve well chilled with chicken, fish, shellfish, egg dishes, even veal.
Red	Red Burgundy (Beaujolais) Bordeaux Red Chianti Rosé	Serve at cool room temperature with steaks, chops, roasts, game, cheese dishes, pasta. Rosé can be served with white or red meats.
Dessert	Angelica Muscatel Cream (sweet) sherry Port	Serve with dessert, chilled or at room temperature. Good with fruits, pastries, cake or cheese.

WINE AND FOOD CHART (continued)

Wine Classification	Basic Types	Wine and Food Combinations
Sparkling	Champagne Asti Spumante Sparkling Burgundy Cold Duck	Serve well chilled. Great with any course: appetizer, entrée, dessert. Fine for any occasion, even no occasion at all.

Wine Serving Tips

1. Wine is appreciated most when served with food. So make sure it's easily available by placing it on the dining table, allowing guests to serve themselves.
2. There is a rule of thumb, as indicated in the "Wine and Food Chart," that matches up white wine with white meat, red wine with red meat and rosé (pink) with either meat. Don't hesitate to break it. Each individual should decide which wine gives him/her the most enjoyment with certain foods.
3. It is customary to serve aged red wines at room temperature (65° F–75° F), dry wines and vin rosé cooled, and sweet wines and Champagne cooler still. The theory goes that when wine is icy cold the flavor is deadened. Again, it's up to the individual. Many people prefer white wines and rosés served thoroughly chilled. Wine should please you; not you, it.
4. When serving more than one wine at a meal, the dryer wine should precede the sweeter one; the lighter wine should come before the heavier one.

Wine Glossary in a Nutshell

Apéritif—Literally means appetizer. Refers to a wine that is served before meals (sherry, Madeira, vermouth).

Beaujolais — Very popular French red table wine from Burgundy.

Bouquet — The fragrance which originates from fermentation and aging.

Brandy — A spirit produced from the wine of fresh grapes.

Brut — Extra dry.

Chablis — A dry, delicate white wine made in Burgundy, France.

Champagne — Sparkling wine. Name comes from region near Rheims east of Paris.

Chianti — A ruby red, dry Italian table wine made in Tuscany.

Claret — A designation for almost any red table wine.

Dry — A wine which is not sweet; also any wine having 14% or less of alcohol.

Fruity — Having the fragrance and flavor of the grape.

Madeira — A class of fortified wines from Madeira, a Portugese island.

Mellow — Soft with some sweetness.

Port — Originally a sweet, heavily fortified wine from northern Portugal. Now there are many American Ports.

Rhine Wine — A term that originally referred to any wine from the Rhine Valley in Germany. In the United States any white wine with less than 14% alcohol may be labeled "Rhine."

Rosé — Means "pink" in French. It's a young wine which doesn't require much aging to be good.

Sauterne — Golden white, full-bodied, fragrant wine.

Sherry — Gold or amber colored wine originally from Jerez near Seville, Spain. One of the finest aperitif wines. Also excellent for cooking.

Tart — Possessing agreeable acidity.

When to Invite and What to Wear. To get the highest percentage of acceptances, give your guests ample notice. Invitations should be sent out or telephoned ten days in advance. Seven days is cutting it close. Less than a week is rude. The ten-day advance period is rather ideal because it gives your guests enough time to make their own arrangements. Single guests who are invited with a date have sufficient time to ask the right person. Married couples with children can arrange for baby-sitters. People who have to travel a reasonable distance won't be caught with their cars in the body shop. Others who have tentative travel plans might want to manipulate their schedules to attend your party. If they can't, you have enough time to find a replacement guest.

Last minute party plans make it hectic for everyone, and are often self-defeating. Better not to have a party at all than to ad lib one into a state of chaos.

When inviting your guests they may ask how they should dress. If attire is not understood by the very nature of the party, then you should be specific. Most parties now are casual. People seem to relax more when they dress in leisure clothes. However, if you have other ideas, make certain that every guest is aware of them. It would be uncomfortable for one guest to be dressed to the teeth in the midst of a symphony of denim and cordoroy.

Unexpected Company. Some people believe in the sanctity of a friend's privacy, so if they have a notion to drop by they will always call first. Others, especially those who live in the same building, might arrive at your doorstep unannounced. If you've ever had unexpected guests arrive when you're in the shower, setting your hair, or indulging in romance you'll appreciate our point of view. Thus, it's a matter of the guest being initially considerate of his/her intended host or hostess.

In any event, if you have little or no time to prepare for your guests, then it's a legitimate "pot luck" situation for them. If you are not well stocked and you do want to entertain (it's not an obligation, by the way) then think of your local delicatessen or corner store. It can provide instant food and drink for this kind of impromptu situation. From its shelves can come an entire menu of quick foods; e.g. breads, salads, cold meats, barbecued chickens, vegetables (canned, frozen, even fresh), desserts and beverages (soft drinks, beer). If you have some inexpensive wine on hand, a wine and cheese party is a possibility. If not, a *deli* buffet is quite appropriate. After all, it's not a gourmet situation.

The Party's Over: Cleaning Up. After your guests have left, it's into the kitchen to do battle with the aftermath.

Scrape waste from dishes, rinse them; empty and rinse cups. Arrange all articles of each kind together. The largest plates should be on the bottom of their pile. Cups should be by themselves. Silver articles should be together, as well as steel knives and forks.

Use cold water to soak dishes that have been used for milk, eggs, fish and starchy foods. Use hot water for dishes that have been used for sugar substances and for sticky, gummy substances like gelatin. Greasy dishes of all kinds, including knives, are more easily cleaned if wiped first with soft absorbent paper.

Washing Dishes. Here is a suggested order: 1) glassware, 2) silver, 3) cups and saucers, 4) plates, 5) platters, serving dishes, 6) cooking utensils. Slip glasses and china sideways into a pan (sink) half-filled with hot water containing soap or detergent. Hot water should touch the outside and the inside of glassware and china at the same time to avoid the danger of cracking.

If dishes are very greasy, add a little washing soda or ammonia. Rinse all dishes in clean, hot water. Drain and wipe with clean, dry towels if necessary.

Places to Go and People to Meet

One of the most vital and on-going explorations in independent life is the act of meeting people who can offer meaningful friendship, intellectual stimulation, pleasurable romance, engaging companionship. When you meet a person who fulfills all of these needs, check your heart and pulse rate. You should be in love. Beyond this kind of very special, deeply intimate one-on-one relationship, each person needs to develop friendships with other people who share common interests. The question is, who are they and where do you find them?

First of all, know yourself, know what pleases you and displeases you. Armed with this inner knowledge you should evaluate people you meet on the basis of whether they meet *your* standards. This is important. Always keep in mind that no one is more important to you than yourself. A simple but powerful thought. If you dismiss it you may find yourself trying to conform to other people's standards. This is an inexcusable self-insult.

The temptation may arise, especially when you're on the outside of a group that you envy and of which you would like to be a member. Resist it even if it means nonacceptance. When truly analyzed, a group that demands this kind of submission lacks substance and reciprocation and doesn't deserve *you*.

Friends of Friends. If you already have a group of friends, the best way to meet additional acquaintances is through them. Although it's not foolproof, the theory here is that you are apt to get along with people who are liked by the people you like. You'll be in for some disappointments, of course. Perhaps even some boring, antagonistic afternoons or evenings. This can often happen when someone decides to play cupid on your behalf. Let's say some friends of yours know a single man and a single woman. They like them individually, ergo the two singles should like each other. Maybe, but maybe not. What your friends may not have realized is that they relate to each of the two single people separately and for different reasons.

If you find yourself in a situation like this and it's an

obvious disaster, bear with it. Put yourself in the other single's place. He or she may be going through the same agony.

Parties that offer mobility are much better. You arrive uncommitted and you can leave uncommitted. On the other hand, you may meet someone who interests you. If you don't, but still enjoy the sociability, then the party ends up as a plus in your favor. Not bad!

Where You Work. You accept a position or decide on a particular college or university based on what it will do for your future. Of secondary importance is the question of what it will do for your current social life. However, in the case of a tie (two job opportunities with equal potential) choose the employer whose personnel composition attracts you the most. It can be disheartening for a young, vital single person to be completely surrounded by older and/or married people eight hours a day, five days a week. Some singles who are turned off by this environment eventually become disinterested in their jobs. Then nothing is gained. But, don't discount older and married people, entirely. They have friends and interests, too, and can be invaluable friends to a single person. In fact, it's nice to have friends in a variety of age groups, children and grandparents not withstanding.

When you're being reviewed by a prospective employer, do a little reviewing yourself. Look around, see who's working there, evaluate appearances, judge the location (is it remote, far removed from areas where your kind of people are plentiful?).

Don't misunderstand us. A place of business should never become a social *watering hole.* Under no circumstances should a company be used by an employee, just as an employee should never be used by a company. Actually, most singles who enjoy the people they meet at a company work more enthusiastically for that company. So everything tends to work out well. Friends are found and work is done.

Traveling. There are two kinds of travel to consider: business and pleasure. Both can produce newfound acquaintances. But neither should be looked upon solely as friend-finding missions. You always seem to meet the most people socially either through business or while on vacation, when you're not pressing. People with a sense of desperation usually are ignored or exploited. You can live without this kind of contradictory result.

When traveling to a location that doesn't offer the promise of easy sociability, one idea is to ask your friends if they have friends there. This may lead to something as interesting as having coffee with a stranger—or as memorable as an unexpected romance. It's worth considering.

Your own out-of-town business contacts may be a good "meeting" source. They might be happy to introduce you to some of their friends.

When planning a vacation (the next chapter will cover this subject in more detail) ask friends, check with travel agents, keep your ear to the ground. There are many exciting places and countries to see. Often, meeting people comes naturally within the context of a vacation (ski lodge, poolside, boats, trains). Travel clubs put people together, too. So they should be investigated. If you're interested in getting a date don't give the impression that you can't live without one. It's a sure turn-off.

Clubs. There are lots of singles' clubs in existence now that offer vacationing, skiing, dancing, tennis, golf, cocktail parties, tours. Seemingly there couldn't be a more appropriate meeting ground. Married people and older singles cannot join, so you are assured of being among your peers. Check the singles' club in your locale. You should get a look at their facilities, members and activities before committing to a contractual fee. Some singles find these clubs to be too high-powered; the setting to be too contrived and dedicated to the *hunt.* Other singles love it. It's a matter of taste—yours, not theirs.

Politics. Politics is a field that's crying for dedicated, young people. If this kind of involvement is at all appealing to you, expect a social bonus. During an election year there are all sorts of volunteers, many of them single, working at the various headquarters of their candidates. The excitement of the race becomes contagious. A common cause abounds and so does togetherness. You're sure to meet some people who will interest you, if this kind of endeavor is to your liking.

Sports. Our society is more active than ever before. Participation sports are now the thing. Besides being highly beneficial to health, they're also excellent door-openers to new relationships.

Skiing is a very social sport on the slopes and in the lodges. There are always people around you, many of whom are looking forward to the same thing you are: a good afternoon on the slopes, and a cheerful evening with other people.

Tennis is fast becoming one of America's major sports. There are many private clubs, but most cities and communities have public facilities. When the weather is good, so are the possibilities for meeting new people.

Beaches and lakes are good meeting places, too. So are ice skating rinks, jogging paths, bowling alleys and parks (recreational and amusement). You can meet people while sailing, horseback riding, at golf ranges and clubs, at race car rallys. Sports minded people can be very playful.

Adult Classes. If you've finished high school or college and are now working, that doesn't necessarily mean that you've learned all there is to know. In most cities and many communities there are many educational and craft classes available to post-grads. You may want to take a hobby one step further. There are courses on photography, pottery making, creative writing, painting, art appreciation, you name it. There are also non-credit college courses which can help you improve your business skills as well as classes in special interests.

Although you attend to learn something new and rewarding, you also may develop friendships or meet someone who you'd like to date. Nothing wrong with discussing pottery making after class.

Your Building. If you live in an apartment building or a multiple dwelling, you're bound to see neighbors who interest you either visually or through bits of conversations overheard in hallways and elevators. Wait for the opportunity and open a conversation. The occasion may arise when you're loaded with packages, walking a dog, when you bump into one another. It may begin with a mere neighborly "hello" or a mention of the weather, if that opener isn't dead yet. What it might lead to is an invitation to a party, a brunch, a movie — a friendship, perhaps a romance.

Singles' Bars. Here you have to be careful. Many singles' bars are like mass feedings and the *soup de jour* is superficiality. Take them for what they're worth. Enjoy them if that's your preference. Many participants have admitted that there is little substance in single saloon society. But some have been lucky. They've enjoyed themselves and occasionally found people whom they've enjoyed meeting. Chronic regulars are usually more interested in themselves than the people they meet. Their conversations are often like most popular songs on the juke box. They're replayed constantly. Don't feel alienated if you don't enjoy these encounters.

Letting It Happen. The essence of meeting people is to develop relationships that offer mutual enjoyment and a high degree of compatibility that will make your life and the lives of those you care for more exhilarating and pleasurable. So let friendships happen and see what transpires. Be alert to meet new people but be selective, too. If a friendship begins to deteriorate because of incompatibility, lack of respect, or growing inconsideration, the problem should be discussed candidly. If the situation is irreversible, then dissolution is the only answer for the sake of both parties. Even if it's traumatic, it sure beats long-term masochism.

Through experimentation and openness and a total awareness of yourself, you'll soon know the type of places and the kind of people that are for you.

AT YOUR LEISURE TRAVEL AND RECREATION

Travel

Americans are born travelers with a natural instinct for discovery. People have followed this urge from the New World to the North Pole. There are archeological links between Egypt and Central America, between the North and Central American Indians and Asiatic tribes. We are now exploring inner and outer space. The opportunity to see and experience new places and people has never been more exciting; the variety of destinations has never been greater. And when you're single, traveling is never more attainable.

People travel for two very simple reasons: to enjoy themselves and to learn something new. What a marvelous parlay — leisure and learning! On one hand you escape from your everyday environment (it's therapeutically invigorating to periodically shake off routines). On the other hand you become your own camera, recording self-impressions which you can summon at will and replay in the years ahead. In a very real sense, travel is the music of the senses. You can reach out and touch a new place, see it, breath it, listen to it.

Travel is instantly stimulating, too, because it can whisk you to a totally new environment in no time at all. You can go from city to green pastures. From one country to another, from one language to another. And you can change climates in a hurry. In a matter of hours, a northerner can be transported from subzero weather to a tropical beach, a city dweller can trade a skyline for a ski slope.

Traveling: Alone or with Friends? Do you want to be by yourself when you're traveling or do you want company? In many ways it's like asking yourself whether you want to live alone or have roommates. In both cases the answer is very personal. Ultimately, you must decide what's best for you. Remember, the object of traveling is self-enjoyment. You're doing it on your time and with your money, so it stands to reason that the pleasure should be yours, too. Compromises are fine, but if you agree to a disagreeable itinerary for someone else's sake, you've started your trip on the wrong foot and you'll probably end it that way, too.

The length of your trip and your destination may have some bearing on whether you go alone or with a companion or group. Quick weekends are less critical than longer vacations. So you might want to take a chance, especially if you have the option to prematurely terminate the trip without great discomfort or inconvenience. Still, you should weigh your decision carefully. An hour can seem like an eternity when you find yourself in very unhappy circumstances.

When you're planning to spend more time and money

on a vacation you definitely should consider the following factors.

The Pluses of Traveling Alone

1. You can do and see what pleases you exclusively.
2. You can have a true *solo* experience.
3. You can meet new people strictly on your own terms.
4. You can change plans independently.
5. You can make unilateral decisions; no compromises.
6. You can be by yourself whenever you want to be.

The Benefits of Companionship

1. You probably won't be lonely.
2. You can split costs and live more economically.
3. You can share experiences.
4. Often, interaction is the catalyst for finding new places and doing something that you normally wouldn't do on your own.
5. Very often it's easier to go places in groups of two or more.
6. If another person knows more about a certain place, language, or people, it can add to the travel experience.

If you decide to travel with a friend, both of you should take equal responsibility in planning the trip. This will prevent any possible bickering on the trip about selection of transportation, land accommodations, or destinations.

Evaluate your similar interests so that your compatibility is enhanced every step along the way. Be candid about dissimilar interests and agree to split up occasionally if those interests draw you in different directions for brief times. Stay loose. Be considerate of one another. Be aware of the importance of self-enrichment and you will enrich each other. The best meals end with people looking forward to more of the same cuisine. So goes a good vacation. It should end with the participants wanting to travel together again.

Planning a Trip. Once you decide on where you want to go, then you must go about getting there. A good idea is to consult an accredited travel agent. Travel agents are experts in figuring air routes, itineraries, reservations, and costs. They sell on a commission basis, earning their fee not from you but from the companies (air lines, hotels, car rental agencies) whose services they employ on your behalf. Since they represent a wide variety of carriers, hotels, motels, guest houses, and organizations, they can efficiently tailor a trip to your needs, wishes, and budget. They're also well-versed on escorted and independent packaged tours if that's to your liking. But to say that all travel agents are complete experts is to generalize. Not all travel agents know every nook and cranny of the world. Thus, if one is rather, or perhaps totally unfamiliar with your destination, you will be deprived of an important intangible: insight. The result may be that the agent recommends a hotel from a brochure, listing, or even hearsay.

Evaluate the travel agent as you're discussing your trip. Don't be afraid to ask the agent if he or she has been to your vacation spot. The answer may be revealing. If the agent is familiar with it, he or she will begin to fill in with details. The conversation will be telling, and if it tells you that this travel agent knows what he or she is talking about, then you can relax. You're in capable hands.

Travel Clubs. A phenomenon of the late 60's, private travel clubs offer some great travel packages to their members. During the winter months there are ski trips to

Aspen, Vail, Zurich, Geneva, and other cities such as Munich. There are summer charters to such marvelous destinations as Amsterdam, Rome, Nice, Portugal, Rio de Janeiro, Casablanca, the Orient. Then there is the Caribbean, the Bahamas, and domestic meccas like California, New York, and Florida.

These are charter flight packages, so once they reach capacity reservations are no longer available. But monthly club brochures give plenty of advance notice. Be sure that the travel club that attracts you is a legitimate one. If you have any doubts, contact your local consumer affairs organization or the Better Business Bureau.

Some clubs will arrange travel loans that can be repaid over a 12 or 24-month installment period.

On the social side, the more substantial travel clubs offer their members nominally priced activities such as cocktail parties, wine tasting parties, group lunches, backgammon instruction, tennis lessons, squash clinics, and more. Other benefits include discounts at restaurants-of-the-month.

The appeal here is to very active people, although the once-a-year traveler who doesn't want to get wrapped up in all sorts of group activities may well find the savings on one trip worth the yearly membership fee which can range from $20 to $30. Initiation fee may be another $10.

Friends. Another source of inside information about points of destination are your well-traveled friends. Check with them as to what to expect, where to go, and where to stay and eat. As with any recommendation, you must consider the source. People tend to travel in the same fashion that they live their lives. Two people can be in the same place at the same time and come home with contrasting reports. So, before asking for and acting on a friend's travel advice, compare your standards to his or hers. If they are quite similar, chances are you'll profit from the tips you receive.

Preparing for a Trip

Financing. The first and most obvious way to pay for your trip is with cash. This way you avoid finance charges which can range from 12 to 18%. However, if this means dipping into your saving account which is accumulating interest and may be difficult to rebuild once you're back on the job, then borrowing is worth considering.

A straight bank loan is one alternative. Charging it on a credit card is another. Check the interest rates. The time you spend may save you a good sum of money. For example, charging your air fare with an airline, in some cases, might be less expensive than buying with a regular credit card. Check it out.

What to Take. Experienced vacationers believe in traveling as lightly as possible, realizing that many items of apparel (socks, underwear) can be hand washed along the way. Others can be laundered by local cleaning services. Gauging just how many items and what blend of clothing should be taken is a skill that is acquired with experience. However, here are some initial guidelines that will help you prepare your wardrobe:

1. Consider the climate at your destination.
2. Determine whether your activities will be formal or informal or both.
3. Choose easy-care clothes.
4. If your trip is more sightseeing and touring than socializing, leave expensive jewelry behind (valuables are always a potential liability when traveling).
5. Work with one or two basic color schemes. This is the old mix and match logic. Sports coats and slacks can be interchanged to create a number of different looks. Accessories like a scarf can give a new look. Blouses, skirts, and pants can be interchanged.
6. Keep your shoe wardrobe down to a minimum.

Shoes are bulky and often heavy. Make sure they're comfortable if walking is on your agenda.

A calvacade of luggage might be in character for a celebrity, but for you it probably represents poor planning and definitely means increased tipping of bellhops and luggage personnel at terminals.

How to Pack. First, choose lightweight luggage; this will immediately lighten your burden. Then, pack no more than three pairs of shoes (you'll be wearing a fourth). This supply is adequate for a trip that will last from two weeks to two months.

Clothing weighs surprisingly little so you should have no difficulty planning a well-rounded, compact, travel wardrobe.

Working with a 26" suitcase, a good traveling size, pack the bottom layer with clothing that should be folded flat and smooth, i.e. slacks, shirts, blouses, dresses, and jackets. Alternate directions so bulk is evenly distributed. Be sure to pack clothing on lightweight hangers. Place bulky items—shoes, toiletries, accessories—on top and tuck small items like underwear, socks, and tee shirts in the spaces. It's a good idea, too, to pack clothes inside plastic cleaning bags to cut down on wrinkles.

When you reach your destination, unpack immediately. Since you've used hangers, suits and dresses can be hung in a closet without delay.

Another good idea is to save a plastic bag, knot it at one end, and use it as a hamper bag for your soiled underwear, socks, hose, and handkerchiefs. If you must subsequently pack before cleaning these pieces, they will be automatically segregated from your clean apparel.

Travelers' Checks. If you lose cash while traveling, it's gone forever. For this reason, millions of Americans—30 million in 1973—invest in travelers' checks every year.

When you buy travelers' checks, you are exchanging instantly negotiable currency for checks that you can cash while traveling. Each travelers' check must be signed twice by you—once when you purchase it, a second time when you cash it.

The advantage of travelers' checks over cash is significant. If you lose them *before* you apply your second signature, you will be reimbursed by the issuer providing that you can positively identify yourself and have a receipt or the numbers of the lost or stolen checks. Thus, the important thing to remember is not to write your second signature on a travelers' check until the moment you are ready to use it.

It's also wise to leave a record of your check numbers at home or in a safe place just in case you lose this information while traveling.

You will be charged a fee of 1% of the total or $1 for every $100 worth of checks. Some travelers' checks are free.

One caution: some foreign banks charge a tax or service fee for cashing a travelers' check. Rates can vary. Inquire before cashing.

All in all, travelers' checks are good for everyone. The institution which issues the checks gets to *float* your money until you cash in. Most get a 1% fee. On the other hand, your money is nearly always negotiable while you're traveling, and it's always protected if you adhere to the safeguards just mentioned.

Customs Information

Exemptions. When you return to the United States from a trip abroad of at least 48 hours duration (no minimum time limit for Mexico), you are entitled to an exemption of duty (import tax) on $100 worth of merchandise providing you have not used the $100 exemption or any part of it within the preceding 30 days. You may import articles in excess of the $100 exemption but you must pay duty on those items not entitled to free entry.

If you return either directly or indirectly from the American Virgin Islands, American Samoa, or Guam you have a $200 customs exemption provided that not more than $100 of it is applied to merchandise obtained elsewhere than these islands.

Prohibited and Restricted Articles. Articles considered injurious to the general welfare are prohibited entry. Obscene literature from abroad is banned. Also lottery tickets, wild birds, endangered wildlife, liquor-filled candies, switch-blade knives, narcotics, fruits, plants, vegetables, livestock, meats, poultry, and pets from an area with high evidence of rabies. Diseased organisms and vectors for research or educational purposes require a permit.

Health Information

Smallpox—A smallpox vaccination is required for travel to most countries, excluding Europe.

Cholera—A Cholera Vaccination Certificate is required when traveling to countries where this disease occurs, usually South and Southeast Asia.

Malaria—There is no vaccine against malaria. Suppressive medication should be taken before traveling to malaria infected countries.

Plague—Immunization is not mandatory but recommended before entry into Vietnam, Cambodia, and Laos.

For complete information on all vaccinations including diphtheria, tetanus, measles, poliomyelitis, and typhoid contact the U.S. Public Health Service. Ask your physician which shots he recommends.

In certain, somewhat unindustrialized countries water can cause severe diarrhea. Check with your travel agent. Bottled water is often supplied for your health. And nowadays many of the better hotels distill their own water for their guests' safety.

Also avoid eating uncooked fruit or vegetables. Do not swim in unchlorinated pools.

How to Obtain a Passport. A passport identifies you as an American citizen while traveling in foreign countries. Some countries require a visa, or stamp of approval, to be affixed to the passport. Others waive this formality. Other countries such as Mexico require only a tourist card and no passport.

You may apply for a passport by appearing before a passport agent at one of the passport agencies in Boston, Chicago, Honolulu, Los Angeles, Miami, New Orleans, New York, Philadelphia, San Francisco, Seattle, or Washington, D.C. Or you may apply with a clerk of any federal court or state court, a judge or clerk of any probate court, or a postal clerk designated by the Postmaster General. You'll be asked for proof of citizenship so bring a birth certificate, an expired passport, or a baptismal certificate.

The passport fee is $10 plus a $2 fee to be paid to the person executing the application. A passport is valid for five years after which a new passport must be obtained.

If you loose a valid passport, you should report it immediately to the Passport Office, Department of State, Washington, D.C. 20524 or, if you're abroad, to the nearest consular office of the U.S.

Abbreviations and Conversions. When you begin to study hotel rate schedules, guidebooks, brochures, and articles you'll encounter the following abbreviations which indicate the meal plans that are being offered.

EP – European Plan, meaning room only, no meals.

AP – American Plan, meaning room plus three meals a day. In Europe this is called *full pension.*

MAP – Modified American Plan meaning room plus breakfast and either lunch or dinner. In Europe this is called *demi-pension.*

CP – Continental Plan meaning room and breakfast – light continental – basically rolls and coffee – in Europe; full breakfast in West Indies (see BP).

BP – Bermuda Plan meaning room with a full course breakfast. In England this is called B and B which stands for Bed and Breakfast.

Since most European countries use the metric system of measurement, a few equivalents could help you. If, for instance, you order a liter of wine in France, you'll get a little more than a quart by current American measure. Here are some other helpful metric equivalents for use in your travels abroad.

Length

1 kilometer (km) = .6 mile

Temperature	Customary Measure	Approximate Metric Equivalent
freezing	32° F	0° C
mild weather	60° F	15° C
beach weather	80° F	26° C
body temperature	98.6° F	37° C

Shopping for the correct size in shoes and clothing in Europe could be a problem unless you have the following information on hand.

TABLE OF COMPARATIVE AMERICAN-EUROPEAN CLOTHING SIZES

Women — Dresses

American	French	English
10	38	32
12	40	34
14	42	36
16	44	38
18	46	40
20	48	42
40	50	
42	52	
44	54	
46	56	

Women — Shoes

American	English	European
$4-4\frac{1}{2}$	$2-2\frac{1}{2}$	34
$5-5\frac{1}{2}$	$3-3\frac{1}{2}$	35
6	4	36
$6\frac{1}{2}$	$4\frac{1}{2}$	37
$7-7\frac{1}{2}$	$5-5\frac{1}{2}$	38
8	6	$38\frac{1}{2}$
$8\frac{1}{2}$	$6\frac{1}{2}$	39
9	7	40
$9\frac{1}{2}-10$	$7\frac{1}{2}-8$	41
$10\frac{1}{2}$	$8\frac{1}{2}$	42
$11-11\frac{1}{2}$	$9-9\frac{1}{2}$	43
12	10	44

Men

American	European
Shirts	
13	33
13½	34
14	35–36
14½	37
15	38
15½	39
16	40
16½	41
17	42
17½	43
Shoes	
6	38
6½	39
7–7½	40
8	41
8½	42
9–9½	43
10–10½	44
11–11½	45
12–12½	46
13	47
Socks	
9	23
9½	24½ (also Cadet)
10	25½ (also Page 2)
10½	26¾ (also Homme 3)
11	28 (also Demi Patron)
11½	29 (also Patron)
12	30½

Traveler's Tips

1. Plan to arrive at the airport well ahead of time. Why begin a leisurely vacation by rushing frantically to catch a plane? Your airline ticket agent or travel agent will give you the check in time.
2. Ask your airline agent or travel agent about trans-

portation to air terminals. Taxis are great. But usually there are buses and limousine services, sometimes free but usually for a nominal fee.
3. If you plan to rent a car at your point of destination, arrange for it well in advance of departure.
4. Many foreign-bound travelers find it convenient to exchange some of their money into foreign currency before leaving the United States. That's fine, but check on the total amount of foreign currencies that can be taken into a country.
5. We've already mentioned the potential problem of water in some foreign countries. It would be good preventive medicine to check with your doctor before leaving. He'll be able to prescribe some medication to take along for emergencies.
6. Take it easy until you're accustomed to the sudden changes in climate, altitude, and time.
7. Leave your itinerary with a close friend or relative in case of an emergency but stress that this precaution is strictly for *emergency* situations.
8. If you wear glasses, take along your lens prescription.
9. If you have a physical condition that may need emergency treatment, carry an I.D. tag, bracelet, or card.
10. Travel with an open mind. Leave behind any predetermined conceptions. Very often they turn out to be misconceptions.
11. Be sure that your home is in order before you leave—all lights off, all appliances unplugged, windows and doors secured, and newspaper and mail service stopped or picked up by a friend.
12. Begin to enjoy your vacation the minute you lock your front door.

Short Order Travel Profiles. There are so many treasures to discover in every part of the world that the words to describe them could be endless. Nutshell descriptions can't begin to do them justice. For this reason, we suggest that you plan a vacation by choosing two or three areas that interest you and that you think may be within your budget. Then, research them carefully. The library is a good source of books on travel and on specific countries or areas. A travel agent can provide you with free travel brochures that should help you make the final decision. Foreign government tourist offices may also have information. Included here is a list of these offices and their addresses.

FOREIGN GOVERNMENT TOURIST OFFICES

Austrian National Tourist
  Office
545 5th Avenue
New York, N.Y. 10017

Bahamas Tourist Office
30 Rockefeller Center
New York, N.Y. 10020

Bermuda Government Official
  Travel Information Office
610 5th Avenue
New York, N.Y. 10020

Canadian Government Travel
  Bureau
680 5th Avenue
New York, N.Y. 10019

Ceylon Tourist Board
609 5th Avenue
New York, N.Y. 10017

Cadok Czechoslovak Travel
  Bureau
10 East 40th Street
New York, N.Y. 10016

Dominican Republic Tourist
  Office
54 West 50th Street
New York, N.Y. 10020

Finnish National Travel
  Office
505 5th Avenue
New York, N.Y. 10017

French Government Travel
  Office
610 5th Avenue
New York, N.Y. 10020

German National Tourist
  Office
500 5th Avenue
New York, N.Y. 10036

Greek National Tourist
  Organization
601 5th Avenue
New York, N.Y. 10017

Haiti Government Tourist
  Bureau
30 Rockefeller Plaza
New York, N.Y. 10020

Indian Government Tourist
  Office
19 East 49th Street
New York, N.Y. 10017

Indonesian Tourist
Information Office
909 3rd Avenue
New York, N.Y. 10022

Irish Tourist Board
590 5th Avenue
New York, N.Y. 10036

Israel Government Tourist
Office
574 5th Avenue
New York, N.Y. 10036

Italian Government Travel
Office
630 5th Avenue
New York, N.Y. 10020

Jamaica Tourist Board
200 Park Avenue
New York, N.Y. 10017

Japan National Tourist
Organization
45 Rockefeller Plaza
New York, N.Y. 10020

Kenya Tourist Office
15 East 51st Street
New York, N.Y. 10022

Lebanon Tourist Information
Office
527 Madison Avenue
New York, N.Y. 10022

Malaysia Tourist Information
500 5th Avenue
New York, N.Y. 10036

Moroccan National Tourist
Office
597 5th Avenue
New York, N.Y. 10017

Panama Government
Tourist Bureau
630 5th Avenue
New York, N.Y. 10020

Polish Travel Office
500 5th Avenue
New York, N.Y. 10036

Rhodesian National Tourist
Board
535 5th Avenue
New York, N.Y. 10017

Romanian National Tourist
Office
500 5th Avenue
New York, N.Y. 10036

Scandinavian National Tourist
Office
505 5th Avenue
New York, N.Y. 10017

South African Tourist
Corporation
610 5th Avenue
New York, N.Y. 10020

Spanish National Tourist
Office
589 5th Avenue
New York, N.Y. 10017

Surinam Tourist Bureau
1 Rockefeller Plaza
New York, N.Y. 10020

Swiss National Tourist Office
608 5th Avenue
New York, N.Y. 10020

Turkish Government Tourism
and Information Office
500 5th Avenue
New York, N.Y. 10036

United Arab Republic Tourist
Office
630 5th Avenue
New York, N.Y. 10020

Yugoslave State Tourist Office
509 Madison Avenue
New York, N.Y. 10022

Zambia National Tourist
 Bureau
964 3rd Avenue
New York, N.Y. 10022

Recreation

Leisure hours are a time for fun and self-improvement. Sports, hobbies, and crafts are at your fingertips to provide physical release and mental and physical stimulation.

Crafts. You're bound to have a creative instinct, a desire to create something that is an extension of your personality. The craft you choose may be as delicious as gourmet cooking or as intricate as mosaics. You may decide to dabble in many crafts or specialize in one or two. Browsing in the craft department of a bookstore is a fast, easy, and enjoyable way to track down an interesting craft and all the information you need to indulge in a new form of self-expression. Stores that specialize in crafts materials abound, as well as stores which sell handcrafts. They're a great source of inspiration! You're sure to find a craft that suits your interests, abilities, time availability, and your pocketbook.
Here are a few suggestions.

Basketry
Ceramics – Pottery Making
Needlework
  Stitchery
  Applique
  Patchwork
  Needlepoint
  Quilting
  Crochet
  Knitting

Textile Design
  Silk Screening
  Tie Dyeing
  Block Printing
  Batiking
Woodworking
Leather Tooling
Metalcraft
Weaving
Macramé
Painting

Collections. As soon as you were knee-high, you probably began collecting things—bumps and bruises at first, then favorite toys, then more valuable possessions that gave you pleasure instead of a puffed lip. If you're lucky, the thrill of collecting will never wear off. It will mature into a hobby that can become profitable as well as pleasing. You can collect just about anything. Here are a few suggestions: autographs and old or valuable manuscripts; coins; rocks and minerals; stamps; movie posters; comic books and old magazines; forms of a particular design you like mushrooms, owls, suns, butterflies, moons, for example; license plates; old sewing tools; tinware; old firearms. The list could go on and on.

Whatever you decide to collect, be sure to plan a way to display it and share it with your friends. Who knows! They just might be able to add to your collection!

Sports for Exercise and Fun. You may want to use your free time to indulge in athletics. It's a good way to develop coordination and have fun at the same time. We have given each of the following sports activities an exercise rating of excellent, very good, good, fair, or poor.

Archery—A sport for all ages and strengths. Little initial instruction required. Exercise rating: fair to good.

Bicycling—An invigorating outdoor activity for everyone. From waist down, muscles get a workout. Good for lungs. Exercise rating: good to excellent.

Bowling—A relaxing indoor sport. Not much strain involved, especially for regular players. Good sport for camaraderie. Exercise rating: poor to fair.

Calisthenics—Programmed exercise. Dance may be considered a part of this. Exercise rating: excellent.

Golf—Outdoor sport that requires concentration, dedication, and eye-hand coordination. Not very strenuous but a good test of determination. Exercise rating: Fair.

Handball—A very strenuous sport. Requires endurance, dexterity, and mobility. Exercise rating: good to excellent.

Ice Skating—A beautiful sport for indoors or out. Exercise rating: poor to very good depending on skater's performance.

Jogging—Grueling, but beneficial to body and lungs. Should be done with regularity. Exercise rating: good to excellent.

Paddle Ball—Handball played with a paddle for more finesse and a greater range of shots. Exercise rating: good to excellent.

Sailing—A very satisfying form of outdoor recreation. Requires lessons. A good idea to know how to swim, too. Exercise rating: good.

Skiing—A good escape from routine to the outdoors. A social sport. Requires skill and coordination. It's a good idea to take lessons. Exercise rating: good to excellent.

Swimming—One of the most active and invigorating of all sports. Requires the use of many muscles. Exercise rating: excellent.

Tennis—Can be very energetic. Lessons recommended. Good exercise for entire body. Expands the lungs. Exercise rating: excellent.

Volleyball—A game of skill. Develops a stronger body. Can be strenuous. Often played socially. Exercise rating: very good to excellent.

Walking—The most basic form of exercise. Stimulates blood circulation and strengthens the heart and leg muscles. (Very often it helps clear the mind.) Exercise rating: fair to good.

SINGLES' SUNDRIES

Pets

Should You Have One? If the most difficult test of willpower is to eat one peanut and no more, then surely the second most difficult test would be to pass up a pet store window filled with cuddly puppies and fuzzy kittens. Nature's babies have an adorably magnetic quality that can warm the coldest heart. However, owning a pet, as appealing as it may sound, is no simple matter, especially for a single person.

Like ourselves, pets are creatures with the ability to love and the need to be loved in return. Unlike us, they will live their lives in a state of total dependency. Domestication and its controlled environment has all but eliminated the ancestral survival skills of most pets. If they can't hunt for their food, we must provide it. If they no longer have a natural habitat, our homes are rightfully their homes. If they don't have the means to take care of themselves, then we must clean and groom them. If they can't run with a pack or relate to a community of their own breed, then we must be their friends. This is the commitment of the pet owner. Pets can provide much joy and companionship but there is an inherent responsibility that exists in an owner-pet relationship. Anything short of fulfilling it amounts to neglect and cruelty.

Are you prepared to take on this responsibility? This is the soul-searching question you must answer honestly before making a decision. If you have never owned a pet before, seek advice. Ask friends who are owners. Talk to pet store people or breeders. Research the different kinds of pets and their corresponding needs. Investigate and compare their traits.

Lastly, if you are convinced that you will be a good, loving owner, analyze your own personality (be candid) and needs. Then, with the information that you have culled from your research you should be able to determine what type of pet will be most compatible with your temperament and lifestyle. This is the most important step in the decision process. Don't fool yourself into thinking that a dog is a dog or all cats are alike. They have different personalities and instincts just like us, as you will see.

Selecting a Dog. Dogs can be friendly or shy; fawning or aloof; cheerful or grumpy; calm or nervous. Some foreign breeds that were initially in short supply but in large demand have been grossly inbred making many offspring high strung and difficult to handle. Watch for signs of hyper-sensitivity and impatience. Select a dog as you would a friend—on the basis of its qualities.

Choosing between a male and female is a matter of preference. Some experts feel that a female tends to be more faithful and intelligent. But this shouldn't be an ironclad determinant. Consider, too, the cost of sex alteration, if this is desirable.

From whom should you buy a dog? Very often a friend might offer one from a litter at a reasonable price or at no cost at all. There isn't an easier way to become a dog owner. But apply your rules of selection very objectively before saying "yes." Any puppy can win you over. Keep in mind that in no time that cute little creature will be an adult. If you disapprove of the full-grown specie and decide to give it to someone else, the dog could be unfairly traumatized, especially if he or she has grown to love you. Remember dogs are capable of giving great love and unfailing loyalty. They're also quite capable of feeling rejection and in severe cases can go through a process that is akin to our mental breakdown.

Pet stores are a standard source for dogs. Check out the appearance of the shop and the attitude of the owner before buying. Be very careful. Some experts recommend buying from a kennel. Here breeding is an art. Thus, the chances of acquiring a very fine animal improve considerably.

Selecting a Cat. In general dogs are more domesticated than cats, a difference that can make a cat more or less desirable, depending on your profile as a would-be owner.

Cats are quite independent creatures; they never have completely relinquished the wildlife instincts of their predecessors. Whereas most dogs will be outwardly grateful for affection and can be spoiled by too much of it, cats are less taken by it. At times they simply don't want it. This is not so much a sign of unfriendliness as it is an innate need for independence. There's another generality about cats as opposed to dogs. Their way of life puts less demands on the owner. To a great extent this is true. Cats are self-cleaning; their spirit of independence allows them to be left alone with less owner concern; they don't have to be walked; they can be left with friends without any fear of trauma. But they do need love and care. Their nature does not excuse the owner from his or her responsibilities. As with all good relationships, friendship must exist. If it doesn't come naturally then you're not a cat lover and you should disqualify yourself as an owner.

When should you buy a cat? It takes a mother seven weeks to wean her kittens. After this period, it's easier for the owner and better for the kitten.

Male or female? It's up to you. It tends to be easier to care for a female as males have a habit of spraying.

If you want to be assured of good blood and are interested in a purebred cat, it should be purchased from a breeder, not pet stores. You can search out breeders by reading *Cats Magazine* or *Cat Fancy*. You can also contact breeders at local cat shows. A good purebred kitten (*pet* quality not *show* quality) will cost between $40-$80. If you're not that fussy, a pet store purchase or a purchase or gift from a friend can easily suffice.

Selecting a Bird. Birds are a complete departure from dogs and cats. Whereas you can curl up with a cat and pet a dog, a relationship with a bird must be different. They need affection like other pets, and they will return it in their own way. Birds, once acquainted with you, may perch on your finger, arm or shoulder. Others may *talk* to you or follow you from room to room.

There are many species from which to choose. Pet stores are a good source. Visit more than one, read books, compare qualities. When you've arrived at a final list, look closely at different birds of that specie. If your choice is a lively breed, then eliminate those birds that are sitting quietly amid festive activity. Chances are they're sick—and you don't want to be immediately cast in the role of Florence Nightingale. It would probably take a skilled veterinarian to bring the bird back to health, anyway.

Be sure to purchase a cage large enough for your new feathered friend. It should have room enough for the bird to spread its wings. Spaces between wires must be small enough to keep the bird in the cage.

Check with your pet store owner or manager about

food and toys. Parakeets love to look at themselves in a mirror and will spend considerable time talking to themselves in front of one A Toucan, on the other hand, couldn't care less about toys, although it has a bill that's as curious as it is long.

Also check about maintenance. Bird cages need to be cleaned regularly to prevent an unhealthy odor. Some birds can be messier than others.

Fish. In terms of owner-pet relationships, fish are the most remote. Fish must be appreciated by the eye and the mind—the experience can be fascinating and calming. A fish tank is a society and can be viewed as such.

Tropical fish owners have the decided advantage of being able to mix different species. They can be lumped into three basic categories: surface fish, middle-water fish, and bottom fish or scavengers (catfish and loaches).

This brings up another interesting aspect of being a fish lover. You're also a collector which means fish are not only pets but a hobby.

Buying Fish

1. Make sure that the fish have no blemishes or injured fins.
2. Consult your pet store owner or manager as to what selection will be most compatible.
3. Don't overbuy. An overcrowded tank community, just like any overcrowded community, makes for poor living conditions.
4. Be sure to buy scavenger fish to keep the tank clean.

Maintaining Fish

1. Don't overfeed them. Two feedings a day is plenty. At each feeding give the fish only as much food as they can eat in ten minutes. Turn on the aquarium light during feeding.

2. Aquarium water should always be fresh.
3. Decontaminate new plants before introducing them to the aquarium. Consider using plastic plants rather than live ones which foster the growth of algae.
4. Don't position your aquarium too close to a window. Drafts can cool the water—fish chill easily.
5. Don't give your aquarium too much sunlight. It can raise water temperature and cause too much algae.
6. Check the acidity (pH) and hardness of the water once a week. Pet stores sell kits to use to regulate these factors.
7. Be sure sponges used to clean the aquarium and buckets used to fill it are free of soap.
8. Care for your aquarium according to the instructions that came with it.

Wildlife. In searching for unusual pets some people consider and actually acquire wildlife species such as monkeys, small wildcats, raccoons, snakes. Experts strongly recommend against this practice as wild animals raised from infancy have been known to suddenly turn on their owners. A large pet iguana that had been handled regularly without incident severed a man's finger. The attack was shocking in that it was unprovoked by our standards. And herein lies the danger of keeping wildlife pets. We cannot evaluate their nature and anticipate their every reaction with the same logic that we apply to domesticated cats and dogs. This violence can be terrifying, yet the animal, villanous as it might seem, is not to blame. Capitivity is the owner's doing. And it is a foolish owner who pridefully feels that he or she has eliminated with copious amounts of love all of the natural instincts of a wild creature. To avoid possible injury or heartbreak, be less creative and more pragmatic when selecting a pet.

Buying a Car

Before buying a car you must ask yourself a few basic questions. The answer will enable you to narrow the field and concentrate on those models that are best suited for you.

1. What is the maximum amount of money you can afford? Establish this figure based on (a) how much money you can afford to put down; (b) your monthly income less all other financial responsibilities. Don't exceed this figure unless you're *assured* of an increase in income at some definite point in the reasonably near future.
2. What size car is best for you? Estimate the average passenger and baggage load that your car should accommodate. Too much car is unnecessary, costly, and unecological.
3. What style interests you the most?
4. What features and options will you require?
5. What is the delivery time? How long can you wait?

New Cars

Type	Characteristics and Comments
Subcompacts	Very small. Usually cost less to run. Convenient for short trips and around town. Not good for long trips. Front seat accommodates two adults comfortably. Rear seat is fine for children, cramped for adults. Ride is noisy, often rough. Baggage space is small. Fuel economy is excellent.
Compacts	Can accommodate four adults comfortably. You can squeeze in a fifth if necessary. Generally, they're three feet shorter and one foot narrower than intermediates. Ride is not as smooth as intermediates.

Intermediates	About one foot shorter than the full-size cars. A good choice is a 6 cylinder model — it only gives up 2 miles per gallon to the compacts but offers a better ride. Four-door models can realistically accommodate six passengers. Trunk room is better, too.
Full-sized	Very good for long trips. Six passenger cars. Good trunk space, but they're big cars and use a lot of fuel and may get as few as 8 miles to the gallon. In congested areas parking is more difficult, maneuverability is considerably less than the other sizes.

Used Cars. Check dealer ads regularly before shopping for a used car. This will give you a good idea of current market values. Ads placed by private owners are not a good barometer.

Take into consideration the car's advantages (low mileage, useful options such as a radio). Subtract from its apparent value any needed repairs. Check for wear on tires, unrepaired or poorly repaired body damages, ease in starting, signs of body rust. If the interior of the car is in good condition, it may mean the entire car was treated with care.

If there's a choice between a new car dealer and a used car dealer, preference should be given to a new car dealer. He maintains a service shop and has a larger investment. Also, remember that a used car dealer gets many cars from a new car dealer. Often the new car dealer is letting them go because they are not completely desirable.

Auto Insurance

Type of Coverage	Description
Family Policy	Protects you against negligence claims whether you are driving your own car or someone else's. Protection covers members of your household when they drive your

Type of Coverage	Description
Liability Coverage	car, or someone else who is driving it with your permission.
Liability coverage is quoted as a series of three numbers; e.g. 10/20/5. Add three zeros to each number. The first ($10,000) refers to the maximum payment for an injury to one person. The second number ($20,000) refers to the maximum payment for all injuries incurred in one accident. The third number ($5,000) refers to maximum payment on the property damage. Recommended minimum by Consumer Union: 25/50/10.
Medical	Pays for the medical, hospital and/or funeral expenses of accident victims. Some policies in certain states may also have wage loss benefits.
Uninsured Motorist Coverage	Protects you and your passengers in the case of an accident caused by the negligence driving of an uninsured party or a hit-and-run driver.
Collision	Insurance company will pay for damages caused by an accident. Many policies have a deductible. Let's assume your policy is a $100 deductible. That means you pay for the first $100 in repairs. Beyond this, your insurance company pays up to the maximum of your policy.
Comprehensive	Pays you if your car is stolen, damaged by fire, vandalism, hurricane, most noncollision causes.

Renting a Car Versus Buying. A car is a most desirable possession, but only when it fulfills your needs. Before dogmatically committing yourself to purchasing one, ask yourself these questions:

1. How often will you use it?
2. Can you park it on the street or must it be garaged?

(Street parking in cold climates can cause costly debilitation, by the way.)
3. If you garage it, what will be the monthly and yearly cost?
4. Will garage costs deprive other necessary budgetary areas of funds?
5. If you intend to park it on the street, what is the likelihood of vandalism in your neighborhood?
6. Can you afford periodic maintenance costs?

If you use a car infrequently but like the convenience, you might want to consider the alternatives to buying one. Renting or perhaps leasing might be more economical and a wiser alternative. In effect, you only pay for a car when you need it—you're not paying for a car that's sitting idle. Of course, you forsake some convenience especially if you are not a major credit card holder. Ironically, it is more difficult to rent a car on a cash basis than it is without cash. But it can be done. Usually it requires a $50 cash deposit and an employment/residence check by the rental agency—apply the day *before* you want to rent to give sufficient time for clearance.

When renting, give the agency advance notice. This will assure you of getting the type of car that you need (compact, intermediate, full-size). During the vacation months and on holidays, cars are in even greater demand. So plan accordingly. Make your reservation several days or a week in advance during busy times.

Surviving a Visit from Parents

If you have just started independent living, the first visit from your parents can give you the jitters, especially if it's a stay-over affair. Now you are the one offering room and board. But you can minimize your anxiety if you get organized and take charge of the situation.

The first thing you should do is establish, with no

misunderstanding, the dates of the stay. Then, estimate your ability to accommodate them in your apartment (home). If there's not enough room for all to co-exist comfortably, then suggest a hotel or motel. You should make the reservations, assuming that you know the local hotels and motels better than your parents.

Next is the day of arrival. If it's a work day and you can't meet the plane, train, or bus, explain the situation and meet them as soon as you can after their arrival. It would be preferable to schedule their arrival on a weekend or on a day when nothing will interfere.

During their visit, plan menus that you can handle. It's natural to want to impress them, but going to extremes will only strain your capacity to function well and easily. Do your grocery shopping in advance. Choose some dishes that can be prepared and frozen ahead of time.

Cater to your parents' interests. If they do not know your locale, show them places they haven't been and things they haven't seen before. Judge your selection according to their likes and dislikes. Theater plays, museum tours, and shopping are activities to consider.

It might be a good idea to have an informal get-together with a few of your friends. Parents are naturally curious (sometimes a bit anxious) about their children's acquaintances.

The basic relationship hasn't changed between you and your parents. Only the setting is different. So don't be artificial about your new apartment or lifestyle (and correct any wrongful criticism of it). Relax and enjoy each other's company. Share your mutual love. The experience can be a mature, positive step in your adult relationship with your parents.

Career Opportunities

The first rule to remember is that it is your privilege as an individual to choose a career that best suits your aptitudes and ambition. A career should never be chosen for you by someone who *knows what's best for you.* Usually when someone takes this tact, it's more a matter of what will make them happy. Nothing is more unfair than to deprive a person of his or her natural destiny as long as that destiny is constructive. The complex inner clockwork of a person's mind and soul must be given the opportunity to express itself in a career that will allow the spirit to flourish. The right career—it can be arduous or simple, unusual or ordinary—offers the most enviable of all rewards: happiness.

Dictation by others is intolerable. Intelligent guidance and counsel can be productive. Thus, when analyzing career choices you should talk to professionals, people with knowledgeable perspective, friends, relatives, and educators you respect. Accept constructive criticism, evaluate yourself, add up your pluses, admit your deficiencies.

A career choice is not necessarily an everlasting commitment. Thousands and thousands of people have switched. The trick is to recognize the need for a change before it's too late. Too many people, because of procrastination, fear of failure, or weight of obligations, have become trapped in careers that are totally unfulfilling. This is a treacherous pitfall. The lure is often tempting but material possessions should never be gained if the price is the loss of inner peace.

Choice should also be tempered with a degree of practicality. Is your ambition attainable? Check out the educational requirements and local schools which offer instruction in the field, the number of openings versus the number of applicants, the time it may take to reach a reasonable level of success. Take notes, even create a profile worksheet. Then evaluate yourself and the careers in light of your findings and choose the one that seems to fill your needs and requirements for the kind of life you would like to have.

TAKING CARE OF YOURSELF

Finding a Physician

Of all the facets of independent life, your health should be given primary consideration. Emergencies, of course, must be attended. But now, more than ever, regular checkups have become an essential element in proper self-fitness. Unquestionably, many lives have and will be saved by this kind of preventive action. We're accustomed to giving our automobiles 2,000-mile checkups. Why not treat our bodies with the same respect?

A thorough physical examination does wonders for the mind, too. It dispells fears, arrests problems before they become serious, and turns you loose on the world with new vigor. When you're A-OK, so is the world.

If you have moved into a new community, the first reference source for a physician is your city or county medical society. Other sources are friends, religious organizations, or a nearby hospital. (It should have a good reputation. A teaching hospital is preferred.)

Although medicine is in an age of specialty, there are still family physicians (general practitioners) available. If an illness arises that requires treatment by a specialist, your family doctor will surely refer you to one.

People of all ages should have their blood pressure checked regularly. High blood pressure (hypertension) is a dangerous condition, but can be controlled with medication.

Some criteria to keep in mind when choosing a doctor are:

1. Location—Can you reach your doctor fairly easily?
2. Confidence—Can you speak freely with your doctor? Do you have confidence in his or her diagnosis?
3. Cost—Is the doctor's fee within your budget?

Hints for Special Groups

Women. As a woman, you should see your gynecologist once a year. (Some doctors suggest twice a year.) At this time, you should have a Pap smear and breast examination. You should learn how to examine your own breasts and give yourself an examination once a month. If you notice anything strange, such as a lump or excessive vaginal discharge, you should notify your gynecologist.

Some women prefer a female gynecologist. If you do, specify this requirement when first inquiring so that there will be no misunderstandings.

Black People. Since the incidence of sickle cell anemia is highest among blacks, you should be screened to determine if you are a carrier. If you are, genetic counseling should be considered.

Ask your doctor for more information.

Jewish People. If you are of Ashkenazi (eastern European Jewish) decent, you should be tested for Tay-Sach's disease. It is a degenerative disease affecting children and is fatal. It is most common in people of Ashkenazi descent. All you need to do is get a blood test. If you are a carrier, you can still have normal children. The important part is to know whether or not you are a carrier. Your doctor can fill you in on the details.

Dental Care

Dental checkups are important, too. Teeth are a part of your body. Therefore, they can affect your health. Proper dental care also has its cosmetic benefits. Don't allow yourself to be the kind of person who looks great until you open your mouth. A smile is part of happiness, so be prepared to flash it during all the great, giddy, witty, warm, wonderful times that lie ahead.

Six-month dental checkups are recommended. Not only will they minimize cavity damage, but a good dentist who sees you on a semi-annual basis can keep close watch on problem areas. For example, if you have had a molar extraction in your early years, a dentist can keep track of shifts that would cause unsightly, unhealthy, and unnecessary spaces between the remaining teeth. Even though your teeth may be found to be cavity-free and in good shape during one given checkup, they will still require some clinical sprucing up. Plaque, calculus, and tartar tend to accumulate and must be removed.

When moving into a new neighborhood, you can search out a good dentist by contacting the local dental society. In large urban areas, dental schools will be able to make recommendations. Local hospitals are another source. A number of dentists are usually associated with each hospital. Your physician will probably be able to recommend a dentist, too. Friends are also a possibility.

Final thought: Before you move from one community you should request your dental and medical records. If there's no time for this, have your new physician and dentist request them for you. These records will provide your new practitioners with a blueprint of you. Armed with these histories, they will be fully prepared to do their jobs and exercise their skills.

One Final Word

Be of good health, good cheer, accept challenge, make a better world, and enjoy the privileges of independent living. It really is super!

INDEX

A

Apartments:
  decorating, 19-24
  evaluating, 7-10
  finding, 5-6
  greenery, 24-28
  household essentials, 16-17
  lease, 9
  moving to, 11-14
  security, 28-32
  singles', 11
  two-family house, 10
Automobiles:
  buying, 200-201
  insurance, 201-202
  new, 200-201
  renting, 202-203
  used, 201

B

Banks and Banking, 119-123
Barbecuing, 93

Beef:
  cuts of, 52-53
  grades of, 50
  roasting chart for, 50

C

Calories, 36-45
Careers, 204-205
Care:
  labels, 101
  of clothing, 102-114
Cars: see Automobiles
Checks and Checking:
  frequent questions about, 121-122
  value of, 120
Cheese, 68-74
Classes, 171
Clothing:
  care labels in, 101
  caring for, 102-114
  developing wardrobe of, 95-97

▶ 211

Clothing (*Continued*)
  manufacturing labels in, 99
  psychology of, 94-95
  repairs, 111-114
  sizes, comparative American-European, 185-186
  to fit figure, 98-99
Clubs, 170
Collateral, 123
Cooking: see Food
  foreign terms for, 86-88
  outdoor, 93
  oven temperatures, 49
  terms, 80-83
Credit:
  cards, 128-131
  checking up on, 132-135
  cost of, 130-131
  discrimination, 130
  do's and dont's, 136-137
  establishing, 127
  reasons for, 127-128
  types of, 125-126

Decorating (apartment), 19-24
Dental care, 208-209
Dieting, 35
Doctor: see Physician,
Documents, keeping important, 153-154

E

Emergency telephone numbers, 32
Entertaining:
  atmosphere, 157
  brunch, 161

Entertaining (*Continued*)
  buffet, 160-161
  cleaning up after, 167
  cocktail party, 158-160
  guests, 155-156
  invitations, 167
  unexpected company, 167
Estates, 123-124

Finances:
  banking, 119-123
  credit, 125-137
  insurance, 138-141
  investing, 141-145
  money management, 115-117
  taxes, 145-150
Fish:
  buying and preparing, 65
  cooking methods for, 66
  seasonal, 65
Food:
  calories in, 36-45
  dieting, 35
  ingredients, common, 83-86
  nutrition, 33-35
  safety, 90-91
  shelf supplies, 79-80
  shopping, 45-50
  storage, 46
Fruits, 67-68

H

Health, 206-209
Herbs, 75-79
Household essentials, 16-17
Housekeeping, 18-19

Houseplants:
  fertilizing, 26
  from garbage, 27–28
  potting and repotting, 26–27
  required light for, 25

I

Insurance:
  annuities, 139
  automobile, 201–202
  credit card, 131
  health, 140
  life, 138
Investments:
  bonds, 143
  broker, 144
  securities, 142
  stocks, 142

K

Kitchen:
  abbreviations and measures, 91–92
  cooking terms, 80–83
  safety in, 88–91

L

Labels:
  care, 101
  in clothing, 99
Lamb:
  broiling, chart for, 60
  cuts of, 56–57
  roasting, chart for, 60
Laundry tips, 110
Lawyer, finding a, 150–151
Legal Aid Society, 152

Loan:
  applying for, 123
  cosigning, 123

M

Meat, carving, 62
Money:
  managing, 115–117
  saving techniques, 118
  tipping, 118–119
Movers and moving, 11–14

N

Necessities of life: see Food, Shelter, and Clothing

O

Outdoor cooking, 93

P

Parents, preparing for visit from 203–204
Passport, 183
Peoples' court, how to sue in, 151–152
Pets, choosing:
  birds, 197–198
  cats, 196–197
  dogs, 195–196
  fish, 198–199
  wildlife, 199
Physicians, 206–207
Plants, 24–28
Politics, 171
Pork:
  baking chart for ham, 61–62

214 ▶ INDEX

Pork (*Continued*)
  cuts of, 58–59
  roasting chart, 61
Poultry:
  carving, 63
  chicken, 63
  chicken roasting chart, 64
  duck, 64
  turkey, roasting chart, 64

R

Recreation:
  crafts, 190
  collections, 191
  sports, 191–193
Roommates, 14–16

S

Safety:
  appliances, 89
  fire, 31
  food, 90–91
  kitchen, 88–91
  oven, 88–89
  personal, 31–32
  with sharp objects, 90
Savings accounts, 123
  Securities, 142–145
Shelter, 5–32
Shelf supplies, 79
Social life, 155–173
Spices, 75–79
Sports, 171
Stain removal, 107–109
Stocks:
  broker, 144
  common, 142

Stocks (*Continued*
  cost of, 144
  listed, 144–145
  over-the-counter, 144–145
  preferred, 142
  trading, 143

T

Taxes:
  Forms, 145–146
  Frequently asked questions about, 147–149
  Return, preparing, 145
  Tips, 150
  Who must file, 146–147
Tipping, 118–119
Tourist offices, 188–189
Travel:
  alone, 175–176
  checks, 180–181
  clothing for, 179
  clubs, 177
  customs regulations, 181–182
  financing, 179
  packing for, 180
  passports for, 183
  planning, 177
  with friends, 175–176

V

Vacations: see Travel
Veal:
  cuts of, 54–55
  roasting chart, 51
Vegetables:
  buying and storing, 67
  cooking, 67

W

Wardrobe: see Clothing
Wills, 124–125
Wine:
   and food chart, 163–164

Wine (*Continued*)
   glossary, 164–166
   selecting, 162–163
   serving tips, 164